T0158805

My Lord and My God

My LORD and My GOD

Annie Ngana-Mundeke, Ph.D.

MY LORD AND MY GOD

iUniverse books may be ordered through booksellers or by contacting:

iUniverse
1663 Liberty Drive
Bloomington, IN 47403
www.iuniverse.com
1-800-Authors (1-800-288-4677)

ISBN: 978-1-5320-0283-0 (sc)
ISBN: 978-1-5320-0282-3 (e)

Library of Congress Control Number: 2016911635

Print information available on the last page.

iUniverse rev. date: 11/30/2016

CONTENTS

In the beginning was the Word, and the Word was with God, and the Word was God. [2] He was with God in the beginning. [3] Through him all things were made; without him nothing was made that has been made. [4] In him was life, and that life was the light of all mankind. [5] The light shines in the darkness, and the darkness has not overcome[a] it [John 1:1-5].

NOTES FROM THE AUTHOR

The title, *My Lord and My God* reminds us of the powerful statement in the Scriptures that most believers in our Lord and Savior Jesus Christ have heard before. It was Thomas, one of the disciples of our Lord Jesus Christ, who made a powerful statement stating: "My Lord and My God." Thomas made this statement when he was confronted with the powerful truth at the critical moment of his life as the Resurrected Lord, Jesus Christ stood up in front of him after He had risen from death and had shown Himself to His people; but Thomas doubted His resurrection. In fact, Thomas said that he would not believe that the Lord Jesus had risen unless he put his fingers in His wounds. However, when the Risen Lord stood in front of Thomas and asked Thomas to come closer and put his fingers in His wounds, Thomas cried; his doubt was removed once and forever. Undoubtedly, Thomas fell down at the Lord's feet and made a powerful statement recognizing the Lord Jesus Christ as His Creator; thus his statement: "My Lord and My God." Now, few questions can be raised here:

> What made Thomas fall at the feet of the Lord Jesus Christ and call Him "His Lord and His God?"
>
> Does God exist?
>
> What do Scriptures teach us about Christ's Deity?

Moreover, a challenging question is, will you and I call the Lord Jesus Christ, Our Lord and God?

Will everyone call the Lord Jesus Christ their Lord and God?

Other critical questions are:

What does the Bible teach us about people bowing and confessing that the Lord Jesus Christ Is Lord?

Scriptures teach that God exists and there is Only One God, but Who Is that God? What are His names and what are His attributes?

Answers to these questions based on the Scriptures will reveal to us Who is God, Our Creator.

"*My Lord and My God*", a powerful statement made by Thomas presents challenges to many people who do not agree with Thomas and who still wonder why did Thomas fall at the feet of the Resurrected Lord Jesus Christ to call HIM His Lord and His God when he did not even believe other disciples' testimony as they informed him that they had seen the Risen LORD! It may be that Thomas received the revelation of Who the Lord Jesus Christ is when the Risen Lord appeared and stood before him. Simply put, the Lord Jesus Christ revealed Himself to Thomas when He appeared to him and to His other disciples. Just as when the Lord revealed Himself to Peter when He asked Peter and His other disciples this question: "Who do you say that I am?", and Peter answered "You are the Messiah, the Son of the living God" [Matthew 16:16]. Upon hearing this statement, the Lord said to Peter that the Holy Spirit revealed this to him: "Jesus replied, "Blessed are you, Simon son of Jonah, for this was not revealed to you by flesh and blood, but by my Father in heaven." [Matthew 16:17].

Drawing from this powerful truth, one can deduce the clarity that the Lord revealed Himself to Thomas as well. What is interesting in this discussions is that Scriptures teach us that every knee shall bow and every tongue shall confess that the Lord Jesus Christ is God [Philippians 2:9].

This was a moment of truth! Otherwise, Thomas could never know who the Lord Is.

How could Thomas, who doubted Christ's resurrection make such a powerful statement, calling the Risen Jesus, His Lord and His God?

Although Thomas' powerful statement, "My Lord and My God," challenges some people's minds, the truth is that Thomas' statement is confirmed in the Scriptures, the inspired Word of God and it is also supported by the miracles the Lord Jesus Christ performed as no one else could perform except God Himself. One example is when the Lord spoke to the wind and the waves and the wind stopped blowing as we read: He said to them, "Why are you afraid? You have so little faith!" Then He stood up. He spoke sharp words to the wind and the waves. Then the wind stopped blowing [Matthew 8:26]. Only God can perform such a miracle!

Other remarkable factors include the forgiveness of sins. The Lord Jesus Christ forgives sins and Only God can forgive sins. Those who believe in Scriptures willingly accept the Deity of the Lord Jesus Christ without a doubt because Scriptures teach us about Christ's Deity. Several passages in the Scriptures refer to the Lord Jesus Christ as the Almighty God, Lord and Savior, as we read in the Book of John and in the Book of Isaiah

- In the beginning was the Word, and the Word was with God, and the Word was God. [2] He was with God in the beginning. [3] Through him all things were made; without him nothing was made that has been made. [4] In him was life, and that life was the light of all mankind. [5] The light shines in the darkness, and the darkness has not overcome[a] it [John 1:15].
- Also in the Book of Isaiah 9:6-7, we read that the Lord is the Wonderful Counselor, Might God, Everlasting Father, and Prince of Peace:

> For to us a child is born,
> to us a son is given,
> and the government will be on his shoulders.
> And he will be called
> Wonderful Counselor, Mighty God,
> Everlasting Father, Prince of Peace.
> [7] Of the greatness of his government and peace
> there will be no end.
> He will reign on David's throne
> and over his kingdom,
> establishing and upholding it
> with justice and righteousness
> from that time on and forever.
> The zeal of the LORD Almighty
> will accomplish this.

This information is real. No one is making up stories to support and point to the Creator. It is important to read the Scriptures with humility, with open mind and a willingness to be taught by the Holy Spirit. No one can teach the Word of God better than the Holy Spirit, Who Is the Lord Himself since there is Only One God Who has three functions: Father, Son and Holy Spirit. The Lord Jesus Christ promised that He would send us the comforter who would teach us about HIM [John 16:7]; John [16:26].

> But very truly I tell you, it is for your good that I am going away. Unless I go away, the Advocate will not come to you; but if I go, I will send him to you [John 16:26].

Scriptures teach that during His earthly ministry, the Lord Jesus Christ asked His disciples to tell "Who, they thought He IS. To this challenging question, most of them stumbled; with the exception of Peter who said to the Lord Jesus that He Is the Christ, the Messiah [Matthew 16:15]. And Scriptures teach us that to this answer the LORD replied that the Holy Spirit revealed the answer to Peter [Matthew 15:16].

Now, how about you? What will you say if the Resurrected Jesus asks you to tell *who do you think He IS?*

Scriptures teach us that there is Only One God; He Is Holy and He Is Eternal, but Who is this God? What are His Names?

Scriptures teach us that the Lord Jesus Christ IS God, Our Creator. For example, when you read in various passages including the passage of John 1-5 and the passage of Colossians 1:15-21, you realize that the Creator Who is discussed in the Book of Genesis and throughout the Scriptures is our Lord and Savior Jesus Christ. The Lord Jesus Christ IS the God of Abraham, Isaac and Jacob. He is God, Our Creator, my Creator and Your Creator. The Lord Himself said that before Abraham was, HE IS as we read in the Book of John: "Very truly I tell you," Jesus answered, "before Abraham was born, I am!" [John 8:58].

PREFACE

My Lord and My God is written to shed light on the critical issue of *Christ's Deity* based on Scriptures to bring contributions to the discussions as many people do not seem to believe that there is only one God who Is our Creator and our Savior. He took on Flesh to come to earth to save the world as we read in Scriptures. Many passages in Scriptures instruct us about the Only God, our Creator and Savior, the Almighty. For example, in the Book of John, chapter 1 verses 1 to 14 we are told a story of the mystery of God's visit to His people.

In addition, in the Book of Isaiah Chapter 9, we read that He was called a Wonderful Counselor, Mighty God and Prince of Peace. He lived on earth among men and was called Immanuel, God with us [Matthew 1:21]. Scriptures are the inspired Word of God and they teach the truth; the Word of God is Truth [John 17:17] as we read in the Holy Bible. Scriptures teach us that there is Only One God Who Is Our Creator and Our Savior; and they provide us with hundreds names of God including, *"Jehovah Jireh, (the Lord Will Provide)* [Genesis 22:14], *El Shaddai (Lord* God Almighty) [Genesis 17:1] I AM WHO I AM," the Almighty, Almighty God, Alpha and Omega; Lord and Savior.

Furthermore, Scriptures provide us with numerous tittles and attributes of God among which, the Omniscient, the Omnipresent and the Omnipotent. Interestingly, all the names, titles and attributes of God that Scriptures provide us with are also applied to our Lord and Savior Jesus Christ. This means that when Scriptures teach us that God is Almighty and He Is Omniscient, they also teach us that Our Lord and Savior Jesus Christ is Almighty, and He Is Omniscient, which means that there is Only One God.

Moreover, Scriptures provide us with many passages to teach us about the nature of God and the works He does. For examples, they instruct us that God is Spirit, He is truth, He is immutable and He created the world as we read in the Book of Genesis and in the Book of Malachi. Amazingly, Scriptures inform us that the Lord Jesus Christ is Spirit, He is Truth, He is immutable and He created the world as we read in the Book of John chapter 1, chapter 14, and chapter 17, Also, in the Book of Hebrews chapter 13. Without doubt, there are other characteristics, titles and attributes that describe God and that Scriptures apply also to Our Lord and Savior Jesus Christ, among which Holiness: God is Holy and the Lord Jesus Christ is Holy. Being worshipped, God is worshiped and Our Lord and Savior Jesus Christ is worshiped. Now, as for the work that God does, Scriptures teach that God is Our Creator, He created us and He created the universe. God created you and me and He forgives sins, He is our Savior. Similarity, Scriptures teach that the Lord Jesus Christ created the universe, He created you and me and He forgives sins, He is our Savior. A closer examination of the Scriptures reveals that there is Only One God and He is Our Lord and Savior Jesus Christ; God and the Lord Jesus Christ are ONE [John 10:30]. This mystery is not easy to comprehend. Therefore, we need to examine the Scriptures and we need the Lord's assistance to teach us.

Despite the fact that many passages clearly discuss Christ's Deity as we read in several passages in Scriptures including the following: In the beginning was the Word, and the Word was with God, and the Word was God [John 1:1]; In Him dwelt the fullness of God [Colossians 2:9]. Elsewhere, we read that "For God was pleased to have all his fullness dwell in him, [20] and through him to reconcile to himself all things, whether things on earth or things in heaven, by making peace through his blood, shed on the cross [Colossians 2:19]. All things were created by Him and for Him as we read in the Book of Colossians: For in him all things were created: things in heaven and on earth, visible and invisible, whether thrones or powers or rulers or authorities; all things were created by Him and for Him [Colossians 1:16], there are still doubts lingering in some people's minds.

For centuries and even today, many people still challenge Christ's Deity and fail to believe that the Lord Jesus Christ is God, our Creator. God took on Flesh and dwelt among us as His name explains "Immanuel, God with us." which confirms that Our Lord and Savior Jesus Christ is God, our Creator.

Mostly, I write this book, *My Lord and My God*, by God's grace, He led me to write it. *My Lord and My God* is a book that I had never dreamed to write, but the Lord by His amazing grace and mercy led me to do so. For many years, I did not believe that the Lord Jesus Christ is God, my Creator. Deep in my heart, I was afraid of God the Creator, and I said to myself that God, the Father is God of wrath and He punishes sins. When I thought of such historical events as Exodus, and the Ten Commandments, along with the Flood and Noah's Ark, I was really afraid of God, the Father. I said to myself that God is God of wrath and I felt comfortable to run to the Lord Jesus Christ to pray to Him as my Savior. But, God by His amazing love and grace, assisted me. *My Lord and My God* is a book that I had never planned to write, but the Lord by His amazing love has led me to do so.

I never dreamed to write a book about *My Lord and My God* to address Christ's Deity for many reasons. First of all, the Lord Jesus Christ's Deity is a very difficult subject to address and I have already written a book about Christ's Deity that was published in 2010. Secondly, I did not want to write about the Lord Jesus Christ's Deity because I did not want to write about a subject that could bring on tensions, disagreements and heated debates.

For centuries, there have been disagreements and opposing views on Christ's Deity. Therefore, I have addressed Christ's Deity based on the Scriptures. Most verses about Christ Deity bring to us clear messages and reveal Who the Lord Jesus Christ IS. I thank the Lord for assisting me in writing this book. The Lord said that apart from Him, we cannot do anything, this is very true. I also thank my family and friends for their supports.

INTRODUCTION

> In the beginning was the Word, and the Word was with God, and the Word was God. [2] He was with God in the beginning. [3] Through him all things were made; without him nothing was made that has been made. [4] In him was life, and that life was the light of all mankind. [5] The light shines in the darkness, and the darkness has not overcome[a] it [John 1-1-5].

My Lord and My God is written to discuss the Deity of Our Lord and Savior Jesus Christ by confirming the truth that has been established in Scriptures that our Lord Jesus Christ is God, Our Creator, and the Creator of the universe who created you and me. The Lord Jesus Christ created the world and everything in it as we read in Scriptures. For examples in the Book of [John 1-5] and in the Book of [Acts 17:24]. As a matter of fact, Scriptures teach that the Lord Jesus Christ is the author of life as we read in the Book of Acts. Peter, one of the Lord Jesus Christ's disciples made a powerful statement that reveals the attribute of our Lord as Our Creator when he stated: "You killed the author of life, but God raised him from the dead. We are witnesses of this [Acts 17:24]." This powerful statement informs us a lot about our God. Moreover, the Lord Jesus Himself stated that He came to give life in abundance. How can one give life if one does not have life? Elsewhere, the Lord stated that He is the life, the way and the truth" " Jesus answered, "I am the way and the truth and the life. No one comes to the Father except through me. [7] If you really know me, you will know[b] my Father as well. From now on, you do know him and have seen him" [John 14:6].

And the Lord even stated in His teaching that: "because He lives, we will also live" [John 14:19]. These passages show very well who the Creator of the universe IS. When I read the passage of John 1-5, the Word of God is clear: In the Beginning was the Word and the Word was with God and the Word Was God. This is clear to me to state that the Lord Jesu Christ is my God and my Creator, WHO created me. The Lord Jesus Christ IS my God, My Lord and My Creator indeed! There Is Only One God.

> "The God who made the world and everything in it is the Lord of heaven and earth and does not live in temples built by human hands [Acts 17:24].

My Lord and My God, examines Scriptures that instruct us about Christ's Deity to affirm our faith in the Lord as God and Creator. Powerful passages like John 1:1-5; where we read that In the Beginning was the Word and the Word was with God and the Word was God and Colossians 1:15, "In Him dwelt all the fullness of Deity;" John 10:30: "I and the Father are One," as well as John 12:45, "He who has seen me has seen the Father," reveal the Lord's Deity. Also important to mention in the discussions about the Lord's Deity is when the Lord Jesus Christ told Satan that He created him: "Jesus answered, It is said: 'Do not put the Lord your God to the test' [Luke 4:12]. These passages from the Scriptures along with others will be examined in our discussions.

The main factors to consider that confirm Christ's Deity and testify to the fact that the Lord Jesus Christ IS God, Our Creator will include the worship issue, the fact of being prayed to as well as God's attributes that include Omniscience, Omnipresence, and Omnipotent. A closer examination of the Scriptures in the Holy Bible reveals that there is Only One God and He is indeed the Lord Jesus Christ.

Scriptures teach us there is Only One God. He Is Eternal and Immutable. He Is infinite, and He was not created. He has Unique attributes, titles and functions that cannot be attributed to anyone else, but to Him Alone. He is Eternal as we read in the Scriptures, the inspired Word of God: "The Eternal God declared that He is God and beside Him, there is no other" [Isaiah 6:4]."

Now, in the Scriptures, we read that the Lord Jesus Christ IS Eternal, Immutable, Immortal and Infinite. Furthermore, the Lord Jesus Christ Himself declares that He is the Alpha and the Omega, the Beginning and the End [Revelation 1:8]. As God is Eternal and Immutable and the Lord

Jesus Christ is Eternal and Immutable, it is logical to conclude that the Lord Jesus Christ is God, Our Creator.

On the issue of the existence of God and His attributes, Scriptures, the inspired Word of God clearly indicate the attributes of God, the Father and they assign the same attributes to the Lord Jesus Christ. For examples, as I already indicated, we are instructed in the Scriptures that God is Eternal and Jesus Christ is Eternal. Also, God is Omniscient and the Lord Jesus Christ is Omniscient. Obviously, God the Father and the Lord Jesus Christ have the same attributes and titles.

As God the Father and the Lord Jesus Christ share the same attributes, could it be that the Lord Jesus Christ is God, our Creator? In the scriptures, we read that the Lord Jesus Christ is worshipped and He receives worship. Moreover, the Lord was prayed to. For example, Stephen prayed to the Lord before he died after being stoned to death: "While they were stoning him, Stephen prayed, "Lord Jesus, receive my spirit" [Acts 7:59].

In other circumstances, the Lord was called LORD and God. For example, after the Lord's resurrection, Thomas, one of the Lord's disciples fell at the Lord's feet and stated: "MY LORD and My GOD" when he was confronted due to his doubt as he doubted the testimony of other disciples who related to him that they saw the resurrected Jesus. Thomas doubted the disciples' words and insisted that he would not believe in their words unless he sees the Lord himself and puts his fingers in His Wounds. This critical historical event that is related in the Scriptures instructs and confirms to us that the Lord Jesus Christ is God, our Creator.

The topic of Christ's Deity or the Deity of our Lord and Savior Jesus Christ and His Sovereignty have challenged many minds. Throughout history, many people who believe in Scriptures have accepted this powerful truth and have agreed that there is only One God who is the Savior of the world and the Lord, He is the Lord Jesus Christ indeed. However, many others believe in Scriptures, but they have selected the passages to believe in and the passages to reject. Moreover, many people have rejected the truth of the Scriptures and don't believe in Scriptures at all. In addition, some people have chosen to remain neutral by saying that they neither believe nor don't believe. In other words, to people in this last group, who say that they are neutral, it does not matter whether the Lord Jesus Christ IS Lord or Not. Usually, they assume that they don't care.

Now, regardless of one's position today, the fact of the matter is that one day, everyone will be confronted with the question: "Who do you say I am?"

Who Do you say the Lord Jesus Christ IS?

My Lord and My God addresses few subjects that allow us to discuss Christ's Deity to shed light on this challenging issue based on the Scriptures, the inspired Word of God in the Holy Bible. The major topics *My Lord and My* God addresses include the following:

- God Exists, He IS Our Creator
- God Created Us in His Image
- There is Only One God
- The Deity of the Lord Jesus Christ
- The Most Difficult Thing to Comprehend.
- A Conversation with the Lord Jesus Christ
- WHO Do You Say I AM?
- Bible Verses that Teach that Jesus IS God.
- The Lord Jesus Christ's Claims about HIMSELF
- Confessing the Name of the Lord Jesus Christ to Be Saved
- Lord Jesus Christ, My God and My Creator.
- The Significance of the Passage of John 1-5 in the New Testament
- The Lord Jesus Christ's Attributes

We will consider Scriptures to examine Christ's Deity and His attributes. We believe that upon completing the readings about the critical facts that testify to Our Lord and Savior Jesus Christ's Deity including the fact of being prayed to and the worship issue that are supported by numerous passages from the Scriptures, doubts will be removed.

In addition, we trust that the reading of numerous verses from Scriptures that *My Lord and My God has compiled* to address Christ's Deity will convince those who may still doubt Christ's Deity to realize that there is Only One God Who Is Truth and Who Is Immortal, He is Our Creator and His attributes define HIM. He IS Spirit the Way, the Truth and the Life, He Is our Lord and Savior, Lord Jesus Christ.

The fundamental question that can be raised here is: Who do you say the Lord Jesus Christ IS?

To effectively answer this question, we need to examine Scriptures because Scriptures are the inspired Word of God. They teach us about the nature of God and His attributes and they instruct us that there is Only One God. Now to determine who the Lord Jesus Christ Is, we need to look at Scriptures to guide us in the search to answer the critical question the Lord may ask us one day: *"Who do you say I AM?"*

"Who do you say I AM?"

This is a challenging question each of us may face one day. I am inclined to say: "will face" instead of "may face" because Scriptures instruct us that every knee shall bow and every tongue shall confess that Jesus Christ is Lord as we read in Philippians 2:9. Now, based on the truth of the Scriptures, it is very possible that all individuals will face this question. Believers or non-believers will come face to face with the Lord Jesus Christ and fall at His Feet. In that sense, coming face to face with the Lord Jesus Christ or standing at the throne of judgement implies having to recognize Him as your Lord, God and your Savior, therefore, you are faced with this question: "Who do you Say I AM?"

As a matter of fact, the Lord Jesus Christ Himself raised this critical question as He addressed His disciples: "Who do you Say I am?" the Lord asked. Scriptures inform us that only one disciple, named Peter was able to give the correct answer to the Lord's question. In addition, the Lord said that the answer was revealed to Peter by the Holy Spirit. There are many lessons to learn here, one of them being that the Lord has mercy on us and He reveals Himself to His people.

Clearly, the Lord reveals Himself, He hears prayers and He answers them. Similarly, if we repent from our sins and we cry to the Lord, He will assist us because God hears prayers. The LORD is far from the wicked, but he hears the prayer of the righteous [Proverbs 15:29].

What the discussion is about:

In summary this discussion is about the attributes of our Lord and Savior Jesus Christ and His titles which include: Creator, Lord, God Almighty, Savior, King and Judge. In this book, *My Lord and My God,* I am pointing at the fact that Scriptures, the inspired Word of God instruct us that the Lord Jesus Christ is God, Almighty, He has eternal existence and is God, our Creator as we read in various passages in the Scriptures in the Holy Bible. For example, regarding the eternal existence of our Lord and Savior Jesus Christ, the passage of Isaiah 9-6 refers to the Lord as Almighty God and everlasting Father:

> "For unto us a child is born, and his name shall be called Wonderful, Counsellor, The mighty God, The everlasting Father..." [Isaiah 9:6].

Even more interesting is when we read in the Scriptures that the Lord Jesus Christ existed with God prior to creation:

> "In the beginning was the Word, and the Word was with God, and the Word was God. The same was in the beginning with God."[John 1:1-3].

Clearly, this passage teaches us that the Lord Jesus created everything; all things were made by HIM and for HIM. When it is stated in the Scriptures that all things were made by the Lord Jesus Christ, it means, all things. As I ponder on this passage from the Scriptures, I cannot think of anything that does not emanate from creation. It is worth mentioning with confidence that life originated from Christ. All man's inventions originate from God's creation just as life emanates from God. In science as in literature all come from God.

Some people have said that some material things are man's invention, yet they forget that the intelligence that men have used to make the material things comes from God. It is not necessary to discuss possible elements that men may have invented apart from materials God created for the simple reason that there is none. There is nothing that has been made outside of God and His Creation. You may try to imagine some matters or elements that exist outside of God and His creation, but as you examine whatever you think was made by men, please be assured that your thoughts will wander around and will come back to God and His creation because all was created by God who is Our Lord and Savior Jesus Christ.

Elsewhere in the Scriptures, the Lord Jesus Christ Himself teaches this about Himself and clearly shows that He is God, our Creator. For example, when The Lord stated that before Abraham existed, He, the Lord Jesus Christ exists.

> "Very truly I tell you," Jesus answered, "before Abraham was born, I am!" [John 8:58].

Obviously, the Lord did not mean that He exists as the first created being, the deep message in the Lord's sentence is that He exists before Abraham existed and He created him. Historians inform us that this is why the Pharisees wanted to stone HIM. They wanted to kill him because He claimed that He is God: "We are not stoning you for any good work," they replied, "but for blasphemy, because you, a mere man, claim to be God" [John 10:33].

In some other circumstances, the Lord states that if you destroy this temple, I will rebuild it in three days. That's deep. He is telling us that He is Our Creator and He is the Almighty God.

When He said that, "I give my life by my own accord, no one takes it by force. I have the power to give it and to take it back;" These sentences are deep and they confirm Christ's Deity as God Almighty and Everlasting God.

> [8] "I am the Alpha and the Omega," says the Lord God, "who is, and who was, and who is to come, the Almighty" [Revelations 1:8]

> [13] I am the Alpha and the Omega, the First and the Last, the Beginning and the End [Revelation22:13].

The Lord Jesus Christ is described in Scriptures as God, our Creator, and as Our Judge.

This statement is powerful and is accepted by many believers who have faith in God and who believe that Scriptures are the breathed Word of God. Now, while many believers accept the powerful statement that the Lord Jesus Christ is God, our Creator who created the heavens and the earth, there are many people who may say that stating that the Lord Jesus Christ created the universe sounds strange and even provocative. Some people may say this because they have never searched the Scriptures or even have wanted to take time to read the Scriptures in the Holy Bible and they even have not prayed to God to ask if He is indeed the Lord Jesus Christ. The best place to start to search for the truth about Christ's Deity is in the Scriptures because they are the Word of God and they instruct us that the Lord Jesus Christ is God, Our Creator.

As the Creator

Scriptures state that the Lord Jesus Christ created everything and He was not created. We read this in the Book of Colossians 1:1-15, and in the Book of John 1;1-14. As the Lord created everything and He Himself was not created, this means that the Lord Jesus Christ is God, our Creator because only God was not created.

Moreover, when the Lord Jesus Christ Himself declared to Satan that He created Satan, this clearly means that the Lord is God, our creator. When Scriptures describe the nature and the titles of the Lord Jesus Christ, it becomes clear that the Lord Jesus Christ is God, our Creator. Consider the following passages from Scriptures:

- "He [Jesus Christ] was in the beginning with God. All things were made through Him and without Him nothing was made" [John 1:2-3].

When one reads the passage above, there is nothing else to explain to indicate that the Lord Jesus Christ is God, Our creator because as it is stated, without the Lord Jesus Christ, nothing was made that has been made, clearly, the Lord Jesus Christ is God, our Creator.

- [John 1:10] "He was in the world, and the world was made by him, and the world knew him not."

- [I Corinthians 8:6]. But to us there is but one God, the Father, of whom are all things, and we in him; and one Lord Jesus Christ, by whom are all things, and we by him."
- Colossians 1:16-17- "For by him [Jesus Christ] were all things created, that are in heaven, and that are in earth, visible and invisible, whether they be thrones, or dominions, or principalities, or powers: all things were created by him, and for him: And he is before all things, and by him all things consist."

Finally, the Lord Jesus Christ is described in Scriptures as the Judge.

Many people believe that there will be a Judgement Day; this is true because based on Scriptures, there will be the last day and on that day, God will judge the world. Besides, the Lord Jesus Christ Himself taught about the Judgment Day during His earthly ministry and Scriptures also tell us that the Lord Jesus Christ is God and He is the Judge who will judge the world. The world will be judged by the Lord Jesus Christ.

Let us first read the Lord's teaching about the Judgment Day:

- "[Matthew 25:31-33, 41]. ""When the Son of man shall come in his glory, and all the holy angels with him, then shall he sit upon the throne of his glory: And before him shall be gathered all nations: and he shall separate them one from another, as a shepherd divideth his sheep from the goats: And he shall set the sheep on his right hand, but the goats on the left.... Then shall he say also unto them on the left hand, Depart from me, ye cursed, into everlasting fire, prepared for the devil and his angelsJohn 12:48-"He that rejecteth me, and receiveth not my words, hath one that judgeth him: the word that I have spoken, the same shall judge him in the last day."

Now, elsewhere in the Scriptures we are told that the Lord Jesus Christ is the Judge.

- Romans 2:16-"In the day when God shall judge the secrets of men by Jesus Christ...."

This passage clearly informs us that God will judge the world, God will Judge the world by the Lord Jesus Christ. A carefully examination of the contents in this passage, may compel one to ask the question: "What does it mean that 'God will judge the world by Jesus Christ!' But before you even start considering the question and seeking for answers, we must first realize that there is only One God who created us and the entire universe; He is the judge and He is Our Lord and savior Jesus Christ. There is only One God who has various functions and various names including the name Immanuel which means God with us. In other words, God is The Word, He Is Our Lord and Savior Jesus Christ, and the Lord Jesus Christ said that His Word will judge the world. We know that God is the Word and the Lord Jesus Christ is the Word of God [John 1: 1:5]. The simple explanation is that the Lord Jesus Christ is the Word of God who took on flesh. This is not an interpretation of the Scriptures; no one should interpret Scriptures. We know that Scriptures do not contradict themselves.

A close examination of Scriptures reveals that the Lord Jesus Christ is the Judge. For examples, in the following passages we read:

- Romans 14:10-12-"For we shall stand before the judgment seat of Christ. For it is written: 'As I live, says the LORD [Jehovah], Every knee shall bow to Me, and every tongue shall confess to God.' So then each of us shall give account of himself to God"
- 2 Corinthians 5:10-"For we must all appear before the judgment seat of Christ; that every one may receive the things done in his body, according to that he hath done, whether it be good or bad."
- 2 Timothy 4:1, 8-"...the Lord Jesus Christ, who shall judge the quick and the dead at his appearing and his kingdom.... Henceforth there is laid up for me a crown of righteousness, which the Lord, the righteous judge, shall give me at that day: and not to me only, but unto all them also that love his appearing."

All the Scriptures above instruct us that there will be judgment and that the Lord Jesus Christ is God, our Creator and He is the Judge Who will judge the world. A closer analysis of various passages in Scriptures indicates that there is Only One God Who will judge the world and He Is Our Lord and Savior Jesus Christ. Scriptures don't contradict themselves. Scriptures instruct us that God exists and He is Our creator, as we read in the Book of Genesis chapter 1 and in the Book of John chapter 1. God created us in His image [Genesis 1:27]. Scriptures also instruct us that the Lord Jesus Christ is God, our Creator and He is the Sustainer of the universe [Colossian 1:15].

Conclusion

Scriptures describe the Lord Jesus Christ with various titles and attributes including "the Author of Life, the Sustainer of the Universe, and Almighty God. All these attributes testify to the fact that the Lord Jesus Christ is God, our Creator. When you trust God and humbly ask Him to instruct you about Himself and you sincerely believe that Scriptures are the Word of God, you will soon realize that the Lord Jesus Christ is God, our Creator, my Creator and your Creator. You will also realize that there is Only One God and He is the Lord Jesus Christ, God of the Old Testament and of the New Testament. You cannot be wrong about this because Scriptures don't contradict themselves. When I was growing up as a young Christian woman, I always felt confident to pray to the Lord Jesus Christ, to praise Him and to thank Him for my salvation because He is the Savior, but deep in my heart, I was often afraid of God, the Father, because I thought that He was God of wrath who punishes sins, but later in my earlier twenties when I learned that the Lord Jesus Christ is God, Our Creator, I was so thrilled with joy.

I remember when I learned about this powerful truth as friend noticed that I was avoiding to mention God, the Creator, but was happy to praise the Lord Jesus Christ as my Savior and this friend commented: "Why are you afraid of God, the Creator, you love the Lord Jesus, He is the same God." "Many people are afraid of God, the creator, but they pray to the Lord Jesus, they do not know that the Lord Jesus Christ is God, our Creator," he added. Those words were so sharp and they marked my mind. Of course, later I learned from the Scriptures and the Lord by His amazing love confirmed the truth and He assisted me. When I read in the Scriptures that the Lord Jesus Christ is God, Our Creator, I was very happy. Later, the Lord Jesus Christ assisted me a lot and He strengthened my faith. In other words, even though I believed that there is Only One God, for many years, this powerful truth did not sink deep in my heart, it took God's grace to instruct me. The Lord Jesus Christ assisted me a lot to believe that He is God, my Creator and my Savior; God Who created me. This is the ultimate awesome and powerful truth.

Activities for this Chapter

1. In your opinion, does God exist?

   ____
   ____
   ____
   ____

2. How do you Know God exists? Please support your arguments with strong statements from the Scriptures

   a. ____
   b. ____

3. In case you doubt God's existence or you don't believe in HIM at all, please explain why you don't believe in God's existence. Also, if you don't believe in Scriptures as the breathed Word of God and if nature does not clearly testify to God's existence, in your opinion, please indicate which evidence you wish to see in order to believe in God's existence.

   ____
   ____
   ____
   ____

Finally, if you still have doubts about God's existence, please feel free to talk to HIM in prayer; humble yourself before the Lord and sincerely, ask the LORD to minister to you and to manifest HIS existence and show himself to you. When you pray to the Lord, please believe in Him, be patient, and wait on Him. The Lord is Sovereign and He answers prayers according to His Will. What is more encouraging is that Scriptures teach us that the Lord answers prayers as we read in Scriptures:

> "Before they call I will answer; while they are still speaking I will answer" [Isaiah 65:24].
>
> Moreover, Scriptures teach that the Lord's ears are attentive to the prayer of the just. The LORD is far from the wicked, but he hears the prayer of the righteous [Proverbs 15; 29].

If you repent from your sins and cry to the Lord for forgiveness; rest assured that the Lord will hear your prayers as we read in various passages of the Scriptures including Proverbs 15:29 for God is faithful and He honors His Word.

CHAPTER 1

God Exists, He IS Our Creator

> In the beginning God created the heavens and the earth. [2] Now the earth was formless and empty, darkness was over the surface of the deep, and the Spirit of God was hovering over the waters [Genesis 1:1].

The statement that God exists and He is our Creator should not be surprising because this is the truth that cannot be defeated. Many people have denied God's existence and have presented various arguments to support their views, but none of the arguments presented to deny God's existence has defeated the Truth about God's existence because God exists, God IS and He is acting with Power.

Instructions about God's existence and His love for the world are found in the Scriptures, the inspired Word of God. For example, regarding creation, Scriptures instruct us that God exists and He created the world:

> God spoke the world into Existence [John 1:1-5].

This is a powerful statement about creation that explains the origin of life. While some people may spend time questioning God's existence and seeking to explain the origin of life by ignoring the Word of God, Scriptures have testified to God's existence and have provided answers to all questions regarding God's existence and His creation. As a matter of fact, in the Book of Acts, we read that:

> God created the universe and everything in it [Acts 24:17]

God reveals Himself to His people in many ways including through nature and through His Son, Our Lord and Savior Jesus Christ.

That God exists should not be a problem because God Is. In the discussions about God's existence and other trends that seek to explain the origin of life, philosophers who have been known for arguing, debating, and putting arguments forwards have taught us some interesting lessons to learn about God's existence.

I can recall here the example of Socrates, a Greek Philosopher who believed in God's existence, in life after death and in the immortality of the soul. Socrates believed in God and in the continuation of life after death to the point of accepting to drink poison to go and live after death. He believed in God in the 5th century before Christ.

For his part, St Augustine of Hippo, teaches us about God's existence in his writings, notably in His volume titled the City of God: *De Civitate Dei*, also known as *De Civitate Dei contra Paganos*, which can be translated into Modern English as t*he City of God Against the Pagans*.

Reading the *City of God* in Latin, the original language which St. Augustine used to write the texts is an enriching experience as one receives the message directly from the original text. I studied Latin in High School at the *Alingba Institute* in Kinshasa, in the Democratic Republic of the Congo where I was born. Latin is easy to read and to write; however, it is difficult to translate a text that is written in Latin into French or into any other language and *vice versa*. While the translation presents challenges, it is an exercise that stimulates the mind and raises curiosity for one to learn more about the subject one reads in Latin. Now, reading the *Civitate Dei* in Latin, I should admit that the text is rich in contents, it is philosophical, and engaging as it informs you about God's existence and His goodness. It also describes the beautiful life in the City of God.

Like most students who studied Latin, Greek and other classic languages, I should admit that reading a text in its original language offers opportunities to seize nuances that a translator may miss. *The City of God* teaches about life in the City of God in opposition to life in the city of ungodly people or the pagans as the texts explain in the original writings of St Augustine of Hippo by demonstrating as he believed in God's existence without a shadow of doubt. St. Augustine mentioned God's existence in most of His writings that include *the Confessions,* one of his master pieces of literary works.

It is believed that *the City of God* is a cornerstone of Western thought, expounding on many profound questions of theology, such as the suffering of the righteous, the existence of evil, the conflict between free will and divine omniscience, and the doctrine of original sin [St. Augustine 4126 AD].

In the 16th century, another notable philosopher, who has influenced the Western academic world is René Descartes, a French Philosopher, a mathematician and scientist who has influenced the Western Philosophy. He battled with the thoughts to deny God's existence for a long time, but he finally recognized the power of God and His existence when he declared in one of the most powerful philosophical statements made and stated: *Congito Ergo Sum,* I think, *therefore, I am*; which testified to the fact that God exists. "I think, therefore God exists." This phrase originally appeared in French in his work titled: Discourse of Method (Le Discours de la Method) when Descartes stated *Je pense donc, je suis, je pense donc, Dieu existe.* His conclusion was that because he thinks, he therefore exists. Descartes believed that to deny God's existence meant to deny his own existence. The phrase originally appeared in French: *je pense, donc je suis,* it is found in his work: Discourse on the Method.

Another important scholar worth mentioning who is among scholars who believed in God's existence, His power, love and goodness and who have influenced the Western academic world is John Milton. He believed in God's existence and he wrote powerful texts that have influenced Western literature among them *Paradise Lost, Paradise Regained* and Samson's Agonists.

These pieces related stories that testify to God's existence. We can consider here the example of Milton's academic work, Paradise Lost in which he discusses the Fall of Man as we read in the Book of Genesis in Scriptures.

- God reveals Himself Through Nature
  For since the creation of the world God's invisible qualities—his eternal power and divine nature—have been clearly seen, being understood from what has been made, so that people are without excuse [Romans 1:20].

- Moreover, in the book of Psalms 19 we read:

  The heavens declare the glory of God;
  the skies proclaim the work of his hands.
  [2] Day after day they pour forth speech;
  night after night they reveal knowledge.
  [3] They have no speech, they use no words;
  no sound is heard from them.
  [4] Yet their voice[b] goes out into all the earth,
  their words to the ends of the world.... [Psalms 19:1- 4].

God has spoken to us in many ways, through how Word in Scriptures, through His Son and through nature.

Though Scriptures, when we read Scriptures, God speaks to us clearly. Most Christians know how God communicates with them and some of them have mentioned that when they have a problem and they read Scriptures, God speaks to them or gives them some answers to the issues or the situation they face.

Other Christians may hear God in the dreams, visions, and the audible voice of God, the angels and through other individuals.

In this passage, I would like to underline the fact that God speaks to the world through His Son and through nature:

- Through His Son:

  In the past God spoke to our ancestors through the prophets at many times and in various ways, [Hebrews 1:1-2].

- Through Nature:

In the Book of psalm 19:1, we read that nature glorify God, our creator. 'The heavens declare the glory of God; the skies proclaim the work of his hands."

In the Book of Romans, we read that that Nature testifies to God's glory [Romans 1:20].

This is very true, because nature testifies to God's existence. Just look at the elements of nature such as the Sun, the Moon and the stars. Do you really think that these elements of the nature exist by themselves?

People from many societies have made connections between nature, creation and the Creator.

For their part, the *Baluba* of *Kassai* in the Democratic Republic of Congo, in Africa express the majestic nature of God by equating the shinning rays of the Sun to the majestic shinning nature of the LORD.

> *Maweja, Diba katngisdi Thiki, the Almighty God who cannot be look at and Whose rays shine like the Sun.*
>
> *Maweja, Mayi Mfuki wa Mukela, The Almighty God Creator Who is Like the Sea from which salts emanate.*

Basic thoughts about God's existence and Common sense.

Scriptures teach that only a fool will fail to see that God exists as we read:

> ...The fool says in his heart, "There is no God." They are corrupt, their deeds are vile; there is no one who does good [Psalm: 14:1].

This passage from the Scriptures makes sense because there is evidence of God's existence everywhere. Consider for example nature, can the heavens and the earth, the sun, the moon, the stars, mountains, valleys and seas exist by themselves? It is impossible for such an organized universe to exist by itself without God, the Creator who directs and holds the world together as we read Scriptures [Job: 38] and [Colossians 1:17]. He is before all things, and in him all things hold together.

Numerous facts testify to God's existence

Scriptures teach a great deal about creation and about God's existence. Simply put one can say that from the Book of Genesis to the book of Revelation, the contents inform us about God's existence, His nature and His creation. The Word of God instruct us that nature proclaims God's glory as we already mentioned in the Book of Psalm and in the Book of Romans.

Starting with the Book of Psalm in the New Testament, one reads that "the heavens and the earth declare God's glory:

> The heavens declare the glory of God;
> the skies proclaim the work of his hands.
> [2] Day after day they pour forth speech;
> night after night they reveal knowledge.
> [3] They have no speech, they use no words;
> no sound is heard from them.
> [4] Yet their voice[b] goes out into all the earth,
> their words to the ends of the world.
>
> In the heavens God has pitched a tent for the sun [Psalms 19:1-4].

Words in the above verses from the Scriptures are powerful. Only a fool will fail to notice the magnitude and the truth of this passage for clearly, when you look up in the sky, you may realize the majesty and infinity of our Creator. The sky is huge, so huge that no one has been able to determine where the sky starts and where it stopped. This is a mystery that puzzles minds! No scientist can tell exactly where the sky starts and where it stops, similarly, no scientist can explain the mysteries of the heavenly bodies. Of course, astronomies have tried, but honest scientists will admit that the knowledge they have acquired about the heavenly bodies are very limited. The mystery of the hugeness of the sky is a mystery that declares God's Magnitude and that clearly teaches that God is infinite.

When I was a young girl, growing up in the Democratic Republic of Congo, the former Zaire where I was born, I was puzzled by the magnitude of the sky, every time, I lifted my eyes up, and I noticed that the sky was without the beginning and the end. At aged 6 or so, I was wondering where the sky starts and if I could walk to reach there. As I lifted my eyes in the sky, I saw that it is huge and I wondered where it starts. I really wanted to walk until I reached the end of the sky, just to see where it starts. Poor kid, I was so curious and I shared my thoughts and ambition with my older sister. Likely for me, my sister was mature and she explained to me that I would never reach the end of the sky no matter what because the sky is infinite. This curiosity did not last long. I have an older sister who clearly explained to me that no matter how far I would walk and reach, I will never reach the end of the sky. Despite my curiosity and willingness to discover the end of the sky or to see where it stops, my sister explanations was clear to me and I never asked that question again. Today, as an adult, I realize that the mystery the magnitude of the sky declares God's glory!

Now, if there is anyone out there who does not believe that the heavens and the earth declare the glory of God, how can they explain the mystery of the sky and the heavenly bodies, Above all, if they deny the existence of God who controls the heavens and the earth, how is it that they can't control nature and walk back and forth between heaven and earth!

When you humbly look at the nature and the order that God of creation has put in place, you can but bow and praise the Lord Jesus Christ, God of creation. The Lord Jesus Christ Is the Almighty God who conquered death. Life and death are also powerful elements that testify to God's existence and to His glory. If God did not exist, how is that men have never conquered death! Only Christ conquered death because He is our Creator. This is another subject I address later in this book. For now, let us focus on the evidence that God has provided to us through nature to testify to his existence.

In the book of Romans, we read:

> For since the creation of the world God's invisible qualities—his eternal power and divine nature—have been clearly seen, being understood from what has been made, so that people are without excuse [Romans 1:20].

Nature has produced numerous signs of God's existence

You can look at the sea to see its magnitude and learn that it declares God's glory. You can look at the burning forest and ask yourself what caused the fire to burn the forest when there is no one who ignited the fire. These mysteries teach us about God's existence.

Now, the most powerful example that teach about God's existence in regards to nature that I would like to recall here that testifies to God's power is the flood! Seriously, do you think that the event of the flood that is related in the Scriptures is a myth! If you used to think so, please think again! Don't let no one lie to you. God exists and He destroyed the earth by the flood as we read in the Scriptures:

> **Noah and the Flood**
>
> [9] This is the account of Noah and his family.
>
> Noah was a righteous man, blameless among the people of his time, and he walked faithfully with God. [10] Noah had three sons: Shem, Ham and Japheth.
>
> [11] Now the earth was corrupt in God's sight and was full of violence. [12] God saw how corrupt the earth had become, for all the people on earth had corrupted their ways. [13] So God said to Noah, "I am going to put an end to all people, for the earth is filled with violence because of them. I am surely going to destroy both them and the earth. [14] So make yourself an ark of cypress[c] wood; make rooms in it and coat it with pitch inside and out. [15] This is how you are to build it [Genesis 6:9-14].

Archaeological evidence testifies to the flood, which means that God exists, He is our creator. God is Holy and He hates sins, and He destroyed the world by the flood because of sins. Noah's flood is a true historical event that took place in history, it is not a myth. To learn more about Archaeological evidence that testifies to historical Biblical events including the Flood and Noah's Ark, the Ark of Covenant, as well as the Resurrection of the Lord Jesus Christ, one can read articles and books that address these issues based on scientific research sponsored by such institutions as *the Institute for Creation Research* to read such books as *Noah's Ark: Adventures on Ararat by John D Morris* and *the Global Flood: Unlocking Earth's Geological history by the same writer.* Also, important to consider is the works of Bob Cornuke and his views on evidence to Noah's Flood. Bob is from the Base Institute. In addition, there are many books by such writers as Tim Keller that address various Biblical topics based on faith and logic to shed light on historical Biblical events. For example, his book titled, The Reason for God.

Conclusion

That God exists and He IS our Creator should not be a problem for anyone because God has provided evidence that testifies to His existence in many ways, through nature and through His Son. Moreover, many circumstances in life teach us about God's existence and nature proclaims God's glory. Have you ever pondered why people die? The answers to the questions can be found in Scriptures the breathed Word of God. For examples, when Scriptures instruct us about Adam and Eve, our first parents and their disobedience to God's commands in the Book of Genesis, clearly the message teaches us about why people die. Also, when Scriptures teach us that the wages of sin is death, we can understand why people die, why death entered the world. Finally, when the Lord teaches us about His amazing love to give his life for his sheep, we can understand that the Lord Jesus Christ is life. The Lord is life and the way to the Father [John 14:6].

Activities for this Chapter

1. Which elements of nature convinc you the most about God's existence?

    ____

    ____

    ____

    ____

2. What elements in nature teach you about God's existence or push you to deny God's existence?

 ____
 ____
 ____
 ____

3. Do Scriptures mention the Only Savior throughout? In Your Opinion, Who is the Only Savior the Bible mentions and what are some of His Names that are mentioned in the Old Testament as well as in the New Testament?

 ____
 ____
 ____
 ____

CHAPTER 2

God Created Us in His Image

So God created man in his own image,
in the image of God he created him;
male and female he created them [Genesis 1:27]

God is Our Creator, God created us in His Image

God created Adam and Eve in His own image. Adam and Eve are our first parents. God placed Adam and Eve in the Garden of Eden, and God gave them commands, but they disobeyed God and He punished them. The powerful account of creation is found in the Scriptures where one can learn about the power of God and how He spoke the world into existence.

After God created Adam, God created Eve

> God's love for Adam and Eve is obvious. God created them in His own image, He gave Adam authority over all the animals and God made man the Apex of His creation [Genesis 1:27].

Another significant issue worth mentioning in the account of Adam and Eve's life in the Garden of Eden is Adam and Eve's disobedience to God by listening to Eve, who was deceived by Satan and the disobedience led to the Fall of Man and the curse.

Adam and Eve sinned and God punished them. Then, God had mercy and He became Man to save the World. The account of the Fall of Man is related in the book of Genesis, Chapter 3 as we read:

The Fall:

> Now the serpent was more crafty than any of the wild animals the LORD God had made. He said to the woman, "Did God really say, 'You must not eat from any tree in the garden'?"
>
> [2] The woman said to the serpent, "We may eat fruit from the trees in the garden, [3] but God did say, 'You must not eat fruit from the tree that is in the middle of the garden, and you must not touch it, or you will die.'"
>
> [4] "You will not certainly die," the serpent said to the woman. [5] "For God knows that when you eat from it your eyes will be opened, and you will be like God, knowing good and evil."
>
> [6] When the woman saw that the fruit of the tree was good for food and pleasing to the eye, and also desirable for gaining wisdom, she took some and ate it. She also gave some to her husband, who was with her, and he ate it. [7] Then the eyes of both of them were opened, and they realized they were naked; so they sewed fig leaves together and made coverings for themselves……
>
> [21] The LORD God made garments of skin for Adam and his wife and clothed them. [22] And the LORD God said, "The man has now become like one of us, knowing good and evil. He must not be allowed to reach out his hand and take also from the tree of life and eat, and live forever." [23] So the LORD God banished him from the Garden of Eden to work the ground from which he had been taken. [24] After he drove the man out, he placed on the east side[e] of the Garden of Eden cherubim and a flaming sword flashing back and forth to guard the way to the tree of life [Genesis:3:1-25].

The story of the Fall of Man has been discussed by scholars from various disciplines including, history, theology, religious studies, philosophy and literature. What is sure is that most scholars who have written about the Fall of Man recognize that God exists and He is our Creator, and that the story of the fall of man is true, but most of these scholars don't instruct us that the Fall of Man caused death to enter the world and that God Himself became Man to save the world as we read in Scriptures, [John 1:1-14]. Even though most scholars also recognize that the Lord, God provided a way out for Adam and Eve and their offspring and that God is Omniscient, and He knew that Adam and Eve would disobey Him, and He made provision to save Adam and Eve along with their offspring, they don't often emphasize the fact that God is the Savior and that He is the Lord Jesus Christ, the Only true God as Scripture teach us [Isaiah 6:9] and Colossians 1:15-20].

A glance at the Scriptures about the fall of Adam and Eve and their punishments reveals that God's wrath was serious and that Adam and Eve, as well as Satan were severely punished. Also, the curse of Adam and Eve was extended to their offspring and to the entire world.

> To Adam he said, "Because you listened to your wife and ate fruit from the tree about which I commanded you, 'You must not eat from it,'
>
> "Cursed is the ground because of you;
> through painful toil you will eat food from it
> all the days of your life [Genesis 1:17].

The story of the fall of man and God's actions towards the Original Sin are evidence to God's existence, the love of God and His mercy for men. Although God made the above scary statements for the punishment of Adam and Eve, as well as the punishment for the devil as we read in the book of Genesis, Chapter 3, God manifested His amazing love and compassion for Adam and Eve and their offspring. Adam and Eve needed a Savior and God became Man to save His creation. Considering the seriousness of the matter, Only God Himself could appease His Wrath. Only the Blood of God Himself could appease God's wrath to redeem us.

We need the Savior. God Is Our Savior; God became the Savior. God took on Flesh and God became Man to save us.

- The Word Became Flesh

> 1 In the beginning was the Word, and the Word was with God, and the Word was God. [2] He was with God in the beginning.

> [3] Through him all things were made; without him nothing was made that has been made. [4] In him was life, and that life was the light of all mankind. [5] The light shines in the darkness, and the darkness has not overcome[a] it [John 1: 1-5].

Nothing is impossible with God

Many believers who believe in God, agree that nothing is impossible with God, as it is stated in the Scriptures. God has displayed wonders such as parting the Red Sea for the children of Israel to cross when Egyptians were following them as we read in the Book of Exodus: Then Moses stretched out his hand over the sea, and all that night the LORD drove the sea back with a strong east wind and turned it into dry land. The waters were divided [Exodus 143:21]. God is powerful, He is Sovereign and He can do anything including taking on flesh to become A MAN to live among us; as Scriptures teach us about the Lord's name Immanuel, God with us. This is very simple and clear that with God nothing is impossible. God is God of impossibility. What is impossible with man is possible with God.

Now, most people who doubt Christ's Deity to recognize that there is Only One God and that He took on Flesh to come and live among His creatures fail to consider that everything is possible with God. When one thinks about God's power and His ability to do anything and His amazing love for humanity, one will soon realize that God became Man to save the world.

Faith in God is very important, it helps us to learn and to appreciate all things that Our Creator has done for us such as giving up His glory to be conceived by the Holy Spirit, His Own Sprit to be born as a Baby in a manger where animals were feeding! What an amazing story! Anyone who still doubts Christ's Deity fails to appreciate God's love. Doubts mess up everything in the spiritual world. When one doubts that God cannot take on flesh and became a Man in Christ Jesus, our Lord and Savior, one rejects salvation because Scriptures teach that there is salvation Only in the Lord Jesus Christ and the Lord Himself states that "I am the Way, the Truth and the Life, no one goes to the Father except through me." As we read in the Book of John 14:6. Being the Way means He is the Way!

Scriptures also teach us that the first Adam sinned, but the Second Adam brought salvation. Now, Who can bring salvation to the world but God Himself?

It is a fact that Nothing is impossible With God.

Many people believe in God, but they limit God. They forget that the God of the Bible who gave a son to Abraham and Sahara in their old age, is the same God who by the Holy Spirt enabled a virgin to conceive and made a Human Body to dwell in as we read in Scriptures that "in Him, -- Christ Jesus-- dwelt the fullness of Deity! What a mystery!

More often in the face of tragedies, when there are storms and calamities, we tend to limit God and we forget the power of God Who can change circumstances in a matter of seconds. One may say, "my problem is unique, you just don't understand how serious my problem is." Fine, but is anything too difficult to God? Definitely not!

Sometimes, we have the tendency to believe that God has forgotten us and therefore, He cannot solve the problem we are facing. The preacher may be preaching the Word of God and one says that he just does not understand my situation.

Now, I remember sitting in a well-organized congregation composed of people from various ages who came to listen to the Word of God by one of the excellent preachers in the area who used to deliver powerful messages when he was teaching the Word of God. On one particular occasion, this pastor made a powerful statement that nothing is impossible with God, and everybody in the audience looked at him like he did not know what he was talking about. Basically, he posed this question: "don't you believe that nothing is impossible with God?" There was silence in the audience. Suddenly, a young woman in the back responded in agreement by saying "Amen." I remember the incident like it happened yesterday. The pastor was encouraged and he said "thank you Annie!" I, the writer, was that young woman who punctuated with the Amen, that the preacher wanted to hear to be encouraged as he continued his sermon. In that moment, for a few minutes, it seemed that only the preacher and I, the writer of this book were the two people who believed that nothing is impossible with

God. This is not to say that the preacher and I are perfect people who never sinned, but the example is given to show that some believers believe in God, but they also limit God.

Just consider a case of a married Christian woman who has been waiting to conceive a child for more than 10 years. She is over 30 years old and is told that God may still give her a child according to His Will because nothing is impossible with God. She may believe you for a while, but deep in her heart she may think that her case is difficult because the doctor has said that she will never conceive a child. In that time the woman believes more in the doctor's words than she believes in God of the impossible. God who never changes: *"I the LORD do not change. So you, the descendants of Jacob, are not destroyed* "[Malachi 3:6]. An important fact to recall here is that it is written that the Lord Jesus Christ is the same yesterday, today and forever as we read: [Hebrews 13:8].

The statement this book and this chapter have made is that the Lord Jesus Christ is God, Our Creator. The question the book and the chapter raise is: Do you still doubt HIM? The passage of John 1-1-5 clearly tells us who God, our creator Is.

Conclusion

There is Only One God, He is our Creator and He is Our Savior. Much has been written about the Savior in Scriptures and all the passages about the Savior instruct us that there is Only One God Who is the Savior and He is the Lord Jesus Christ.

Activities for the chapter

1. What are the names of God according to the Scriptures in the Holy Bible?

____

____

____

____

2. Which names of God have really touched your heart?

___
___
___
___

3. Write down all the passages of the Scriptures that inform us about the Savior and underline the passages that touch your heart.

___
___
___
___

4. According to Scriptures is there ONE Savior or more than One Savior of the world?

___
___
___
___

5. Who Is the Savior the Scriptures mention?

___
___
___
___

CHAPTER 3

There is Only One God

> Hear, O Israel: The LORD our God, the LORD is one [Deuteronomy 6:4].

That God exists and He is our Creator should not be a problem or a challenging issue in any one's mind because God exists, He is our Creator and He has manifested Himself in many ways including through His Son, as we read in the Book of Hebrews chapter 1:1-4] and in the Book of Romans [1:20].

> In the past God spoke to our ancestors through the prophets at many times and in various ways, [2] but in these last days he has spoken to us by his Son, whom he appointed heir of all things, and through whom also he made the universe. [3] The Son is the radiance of God's glory and the exact representation of his being, sustaining all things by his powerful word. After he had provided purification for sins, he sat down at the right hand of the Majesty in heaven [Hebrews 1:1-3].

This is the fundamental truth of life because a person who does not believe in God's existence, questions his or her own existence and seeks to deny his own existence which may lead others to say that a person who denies God's existence is out of his mind as scriptures teach.

> The fool says in his heart,
> "There is no God."
> They are corrupt, and their ways are vile;
> there is no one who does good [Psalm 53:1].

Elsewhere, in the Book of Psalms we read:

> For the director of music. Of David. The fool says in his heart, "There is no God." They are corrupt, their deeds are vile; there is no one who does good [Psalms 14:1].

Now, in addition, to this unchallenged truth about God's existence, one thing is also clear, there is Only One God as Scriptures, the inspired Word of God teaches.

> Before Me there was no God formed, And there will be none after Me." Isaiah [43:10]

> "I am God, and there is no other; *I am* God, and there is no one like Me" Isaiah 46:9

- There is only One God and God does share His glory with another.

Scriptures teach us that God does not share His glory with another and that God is a jealous God. For examples, Scriptures teach us that God hates idolatry and we are to worship HIM alone.

> Do not worship any other god, for the LORD, whose name is Jealous, is a jealous God [Exodus 34:14].

> for the LORD your God, who is among you, is a jealous God and his anger will burn against you, and he will destroy you from the face of the land [Deuteronomy 6:15].

- God Is a Jealous God.

In addition, God said that He will not give His Glory to another.

> "I am the Lord; that is my name!
> I will not yield my glory to another
> or my praise to idols [Isaiah 42:8].

There are many that teach that there is only One God.

These few examples clearly teach us that God is a Jealous God and that there is Only One God who is to be worshipped.

Yet, in the Book of Hebrews we read:

And again, when God brings his firstborn into the world, he says,

> "*Let all God's angels worship him.*"[c]
> [7] In speaking of the angels he says,
> "He makes his angels spirits,
> and his servants flames of fire."[d]
> [8] But about the Son he says,
> "*Your throne, O God, will last for ever and ever;*
> *a scepter of justice will be the scepter of your kingdom.*
> [9] *You have loved righteousness and hated wickedness;*
> *therefore God, your God, has set you above your companions*
> *by anointing you with the oil of joy.*"[e]
> [10] He also says,
> "*In the beginning, Lord, you laid the foundations of the earth,*
> *and the heavens are the work of your hands.*
> [11] *They will perish, but you remain;*
> *they will all wear out like a garment.*
> [12] *You will roll them up like a robe;*
> *like a garment they will be changed.*
> *But you remain the same,*
> *and your years will never end.*"[f]
> [13] To which of the angels did God ever say,
> "Sit at my right hand
> *until I make your enemies*
> *a footstool for your feet*"[g]?...
> [Hebrews 1:6-13].

Throughout the Bible, there are many passages that teach us that there is Only One God. For examples, we can consider the following passages from Scriptures that instruct us that there is Only One God. The Only One God Who is Our Father, has three functions: the Father, the Son and the Holy Spirit.

Furthermore, during His earthly ministry, the Lord Jesus Christ spoke about the Only One God.

- The Lord Jesus teaches that He and the Father are One:

  [John 10:30].

- Elsewhere, the Lord states that whoever has seen HIM, has seen the Father.

  The one who looks at me is seeing the one who sent me [John 12:45].

- The one God: Father, Son, and Holy Spirit

Clearly, these passages from the Scriptures teach us about the One and Only One God and confirm that the Father, the Son and the Holy Spirit are ONE.

After reading the verses above from the Scriptures, it is clear that the Bible teaches us that there is Only One God who has three functions: The Father the Son and the Holt Spirit.

The Lord Jesus teaches that He and the Father are One:

> I and the Father are ONE [John 10:30].

Elsewhere, the Lord states that whoever has seen HIM, has seen the Father.

> The one who looks at me is seeing the one who sent me [John 12:45].

Many passages in the Scriptures teach us about the Only One God. Please consider the passages from the Scriptures in the lines below:

- “there is no one like Yahweh our God.” Exodus 8:10.

How clear, one would like this passage to be? How explicit one would like this passage to be! There is no one like Yahweh, means, there is no One Like Yahweh. This exclusion of no other God, but Yahweh, should put an end to all discussions and confusions about Christ's Deity.

- "Yahweh, He is God; there is no other besides Him." Deuteronomy 4:35

Here is another passage from the Old Testament that make things clearer!

> I am the LORD, and there is no other;
> apart from me there is no God. Isaiah [45:5].

This passage from the Old Testaments has made it clear to us about the Oneness of God. There is no doubt that there is Only One God.

- "Yahweh, He is God in heaven above and on the earth below; there is no other" [Deuteronomy 4:39].

We all know that the heaven belongs to God, it is His residence. Now, if the Lord Jesus Christ instructs us that He came from above and He went back to heaven, this makes it clear that He is God because there is Only One God who reigns in heaven.

- "See now that I, I am He, And there is no god besides Me" Deuteronomy 32:39
- "Hear, O Israel! Yahweh is our God, Yahweh is one!" Deuteronomy 6:4
- "You are great, O Lord God; for there is none like You, and there is no God besides You" 2 Samuel 7:22
- "For who is God, besides Yahweh? And who is a rock, besides our God?" 2 Samuel 22:32.

Let us consider the following passage:

- "Hear, O Israel! Yahweh is our God, Yahweh is one!" Deuteronomy 6:4

This passage, clearly explains that there no other God besides Yahweh. I am not sure, how this passage can be explained otherwise! It is very clear and it is self-explanatory. There are many passages similar to this one with few words in one line that get to the point. There is no other God than Yahweh. In other words, there is only One Yahweh! Similar passages can be found in the Books of Kings, the Book of Chronicles and in the Book of Isaiah. Consider for examples the passages from the Books I have just mentioned including the following:

- "Yahweh is God; there is no one else" [1 Kings 8:60].

Honestly speaking, this passage is very clear and self-explanatory, just like the passage of Deuteronomy 4:35, which we read before. In my opinion, it is not question of proving the truth of the Scriptures, rather what I am trying to establish here is the fact that Scriptures, the inspired Word of God clearly teach us about the existence of the Only One God. This clarity and exclusiveness of other deity make it clear that there is Only One Sovereign God, He is The Lord Jesus Christ, God our Creator and Our Savior [John 1:1-14]; Colossian 1:15-21].

The subject of the existence of the Only One God is a serious topic that is explained throughout the Scriptures with clarity to suppress all doubts. Moreover, when the Lord Jesus Christ Himself teaches that there is Only One God, we should believe in the Lord. For example the Lord states:

> I told you that you would die in your sins; if you do not believe that I am he, you will indeed die in your sins [John 8:24].

Elsewhere, the Lord said: I and the Father are one." [John 10:30].

Take a look at other passages from the Scriptures such as the following:

- "You are the God, You alone, of all the kingdoms of the earth." 2 Kings 19:15
- "O Lord, there is none like You, nor is there any God besides You" 1 Chronicles 17:20
- "You alone are Yahweh." Nehemiah 9:6

- "For who is God, but Yahweh? And who is a rock, except our God." Psalm 18:31
- "You alone, Lord, are God." Isaiah 37:20
- "Before Me there was no God formed, And there will be none after Me." Isaiah 43:10
- "'I am the first and I am the last, And there is no God besides Me." Isaiah 44:6
- "Is there any God besides Me, Or is there any *other* Rock? I know of none." Isaiah 44:8
- "I am Yahweh, and there is no other; Besides Me there is no God." Isaiah 45:5
- "Surely, God is with you, and there is none else, No other God." Isaiah 45:14
- "I am Yahweh, and there is none else." [Isaiah 45:18].

Let us believe in Scriptures as they instruct us that there is Only One God and He is Our Lord and Savior Jesus Christ. Obviously, there is no need to interpret the passages mentioned above. As Scriptures are clear on the topic of the existence of the Only One God, it seems logical to consider more Scriptures as they teach the truth to confirm that God exists indeed and He is the Only Creator of the universe. While most passages from the Scriptures that teach about the ONLY ONE GOD and that *My Lord and My God* has considered seem repetitive, the truth of the matter is that reading different passages from the Scriptures about the ONLY ONE GOD confirms the truth and writes the truth on our hearts. I have grouped various passages from the Scriptures to allow the audience to read and to compare them. As one reads, one will notice that most passages from the Old Testament refer to the LORD as Yahweh, and underline that there is Only One God. Consider for examples the passages from the Book of Isaiah when God Himself speaks:

- "Is it not I, Yahweh? And there is no other God besides Me, A righteous God and a Savior; There is none except Me." Isaiah 45:21
- "I am God, and there is no other; *I am* God, and there is no one like Me." Isaiah 46:9
- ""The foremost is, 'Hear, O Israel! The Lord our God is one Lord;" Mark 12:29

- "you do not seek the glory that is from the one and only God?" John 5:44

Now, when we consider the New Testament, the Lord Jesus Christ teaches us that He IS One with God the Father.

- "I and the Father are one." John 10:30
- "This is eternal life, that they may know You, the only true God" John 17:3
- "The glory which You have given Me I have given to them, that they may be one, just as We are one." John 17:22

Elsewhere, in the New Testament, we read:

- "since indeed God is one. Romans 3:30
- "to the only wise God, Amen." Romans 16:27
- "there is no God but one." 1 Corinthians 8:4
- "yet for us there is *but* one God, the Father, from whom are all things and we *exist* for Him; and one Lord, Jesus Christ, by whom are all things, and we *exist* through Him." 1 Corinthians 8:6
- Now to the King eternal, immortal, invisible, the only God" 1 Timothy 1:17

Let us believe in Scriptures as they teach us that there IS Only ONE God, our Creator, the Sustainer of the Universe and His name is Immanuel, God with us, Our Lord and Savior Jesus Christ.

Conclusion

Scriptures teach us that there is only One God, as we read in numerous verses in the Old Testament as well as the passages in the New Testament. We are always reminded in Scriptures that there is Only One God as we read: "Hear, O Israel: The LORD our God, the LORD is one" [Deuteronomy 6:4].

Activities for this chapter

1. Which verse (s) in the Scriptures convince (s) you about the One God's existence?

   ____
   ____
   ____
   ____

2. In your opinion, how many Gods, the Creator, do you believe exist, and which one do you think deserves the Glory according to the Scriptures in the Holy Bible?

   ____
   ____
   ____
   ____

CHAPTER 4

The Deity of the Lord Jesus Christ

> In the beginning was the Word, and the Word was with God, and the Word was God. [2] He was with God in the beginning. [3] Through him all things were made; without him nothing was made that has been made. [4] In him was life, and that life was the light of all mankind. [5] The light shines in the darkness, and the darkness has not overcome[a] it [John 1-1-5].

Scriptures are the inspired word of God: All Scripture is God-breathed and is useful for teaching, rebuking, correcting and training in righteousness [2 Timothy 2:16] and they teach us about God, His nature, His Word and His commandments. The Word of God is truth and the Word of God is our Lord and Savior Jesus Christ [John 17:17; John 1:1-14]. From the Book of Genesis in the Old Testament to the Book of Revelation in the New Testament, Scriptures teach us about Christ's Deity; the Deity of Our Lord and Savior Jesus Christ. People who have studied Scriptures or people who have been reading Scriptures with spiritual insight can testify to the truth that Scriptures teach the Word of God and that they speak about the Lord Jesus Christ from the Book of Genesis to the Book of Revelation.

Now, when you believe in God and you believe that Scriptures in the Holy Bible are His Word, you will notice that there is Only One God, He is Our Creator and each book of the Scriptures speaks about HIM. All passages in each book of the Bible present an account which is related to God, our Creator.

Some people have difficulties to accept the truth that Scriptures speak about the Lord Jesus Christ from Genesis to Revelation; but they believe that Scriptures are the Word of God. Now, since Scriptures are the Word of

God, and the Lord Jesus Christ is the Word of God as we read in the passage above from the Book of [John 1:1-5], we can conclude that Scriptures speak about the Lord Jesus Christ based on logic and common sense, before we even consider the spiritual aspect about the truth that all Scriptures speak about Our Lord and Savior Jesus Christ. Most people have difficulties to believe in the truth even when the truth is obvious. As a matter of fact, we can recall here the scenario when, during His earthly ministry, the Lord took the scroll, showed it to people and informed them that the Scriptures they were reading were written about Him. Obviously, some people did not seem to realize that the Author of the Scriptures was present among them.

Now, when Scriptures teach us that the Lord Jesus Christ is Eternal Life and He is the Author of life, we can but conclude that all Scriptures speak about HIM. Since the Lord Jesus Is the Author who inspired the writers to write about HIM, it is clear that the Lord Jesus Christ is the Holy Spirit and He is God, our Creator. I remember when discussing with one preacher about the truth that all the books of the Bible speak about the Lord Jesus Christ, but in his opinion, he did not quite believe that then he said to me that in some books of the Holy Bible such as in the book of Ruth, there is no mention of the Name of the Lord Jesus Christ. I remained quiet, but I did not believe him because at that time, he failed to see that the typology, analogy, and symbols in the Book of Ruth as Boaz redeeming Ruth, the Moabite as a symbol of Our Lord and Savior Jesus Christ redeemed us from the Original Sin and from all sins to give us Eternal life. The Lord Jesus Christ is Eternal Life and Only Him can give us eternal Life. The preacher did not even seem to see the significance of the Book of Ruth in regards to our redemption because it is through the children of Ruth that our Redeemer came to earth as we read in the Genealogy of Jesus, the Son of David, and David, the Son of Jesse…:

The Genealogy of Jesus the Messiah

1 This is the genealogy[a] of Jesus the Messiah[b] the son of David, the son of Abraham:

[2] Abraham was the father of Isaac,
Isaac the father of Jacob,
Jacob the father of Judah and his brothers,

> [3] Judah the father of Perez and Zerah, whose mother was Tamar,
> Perez the father of Hezron,
> Hezron the father of Ram,
>
> [4] Ram the father of Amminadab,
> Amminadab the father of Nahshon,
> Nahshon the father of Salmon,
>
> [5] Salmon the father of Boaz, whose mother was Rahab,
> Boaz the father of Obed, whose mother was Ruth,
> Obed the father of Jesse,
>
> [6] and Jesse the father of King David [Matthew 1:1-6].

All Scriptures speak about the Lord Jesus Christ because He Is God, Our Creator.

Christ's Deity can be seen in many passages of the Scriptures including in the passages of John 1:1-5; Colossians 1:15- 20; John 14:30; and in Hebrews 1:6 to mention these.

The analysis of Colossians 1:15-20 clearly reveals the Lord Jesus' Deity.

> The Son is the image of the invisible God, the firstborn over all creation. [16] For in him all things were created: things in heaven and on earth, visible and invisible, whether thrones or powers or rulers or authorities; all things have been created through him and for him. [17] *He is before all things, and in him all things hold together.* [18] And he is the head of the body, the church; he is the beginning and the firstborn from among the dead, so that in everything he might have the supremacy. [19] For God was pleased to have all his fullness dwell in him, [20] and through him to reconcile to himself all things, whether things on earth or things in heaven, by making peace through his blood, shed on the cross [Colossians 1:15-20].

The Supremacy of the Son of God, as we read in the passage above and in other various passages in the Scriptures confirms Christ's Deity.

If the Lord Jesus Christ was not God in the flesh, He could not redeem mankind. God's plan of redemption required a clean sacrifice. There was a need for the BEING who has never sinned and a person who was not created, the HOLY BEING. There was a need for a person who was not created and who never sinned because all creatures were under the curse that God pronounced to Adam and Eve after the Fall, after they had disobeyed Him in the Garden of Eden. Scriptures teach us that all have sinned and are under the curse and that if someone says that he has never sinned, he is a liar. Scriptures also teach us that the Lord Jesus Christ has never sinned. HE IS HOLY! Only God Is Holy and He has never sinned, the Lord Jesus Christ is God, Our Creator.

- His blood was the Blood of God: "Feed the church of GOD, which he hath purchased with his own blood." [Acts 20:28].

The Lord Jesus Christ Is God, Our Creator. He created us in His image. The Lord Jesus Christ created you and me, and He created the entire universe [John 1:1-5; Genesis 1, 2, 3]. If Our Lord and Savior Jesus Christ was not God, Our Creator, He could not redeem us and save the world from its sins. The Lord Jesus Christ bought our salvation with His Precious Blood.

- The Lord Jesus is the Holy One. In the book of Luke
- He never sinned:

  You know that he appeared to take away sins, and in him there is no sin. [1 John 3:5]

  God made him who had no sin to be sin for us, so that in him we might become the righteousness of God. [2 Corinthians 5:21].

  For we do not have a high priest who is unable to sympathize with our weaknesses, but one who in every respect has been tempted as we are, yet without sin [Hebrews 4:15

  We were purchased with Precious Blood of Christ, He IS HOLY, like a lamb without blemish or spot.

The fact that the Lord Jesus Christ has never sinned, makes it clear that He is God, our Creator. Let us reflect on this fact for a moment. Sin is said to be the transgression of the law, according to the Scriptures. Scriptures also teach us that all have sinned. Now, if all have sinned and ONLY the Lord Jesus Christ has never sinned, clearly He is God, Our Creator. The Lord Jesus Christ asked the crowd: "Can any of you prove me guilty of sin? If I am telling the truth, why don't you believe me? "[John 8:46].

Also, the Lord Jesus Christ is called the HOLY ONE! This means that He is God. For example, in the Book of Luke, it is written about the Lord Jesus Christ as the Holy ONE:

2 Corinthians 5:21

Yes, "he who knew no sin was counted as sin in order that we might become the righteousness of God." So he knew no sin.

During his earthly ministry, the Lord challenged the Pharisees who tried to accuse him and He asked them a powerful question that blows their minds as we read:

Yes, "who can charge me of any sin?" to the Pharisees. And they're not able to bring any charge against him.

In Him there was no deceit.

1 Peter 2:22: "In him there was no deceit." "When he was reviled he did not revile in return," and "there was no deceit in his mouth."

Our Lord and Savior Jesus Christ never sinned. The Lord Jesus Christ is God, Our creator, only God has never sinned.

The Lord Jesus Christ was without sin. He needed to be a spotless lamb in order to redeem us from the original sin.

My father and I are ONE [John 10:30].

Many passages from Scriptures teach us about Christ Deity and they underline that the Lord Jesus Christ is God, Our Creator and our Savior, the Only Savior of the world.

For examples, He was worshipped, and prayed to as we read in the following passages from the Scriptures. Please consider the following passages that teach us about Christ's Deity:

- Bible verses that Show that Jesus is Divine

There are many Biblical verses that show us that the Lord Jesus Christ IS God, Our Creator. Among these passages from the Scriptures are the following passages that give us powerful indication of Christ's Deity': In the beginning was the Word and the Word was with God and the Word was God… [John 1:1-5]; Before Abraham is, I AM [John 8:58] and I and the Father are ONE [John 10:30].

Establishing an agreement on the Deity or the Divinity of our Lord Jesus Christ is essential if not critical for one's salvation because the Lord Himself said to the crow: " I told you that you would die in your sins; if you do not believe that I am he, you will indeed die in your sins." [John 8:24]. The Lord stated that He is the Way, the Truth and the Life and that no one goes to the Farther except through Him [John 14:6]. So, believing in Him is critical for salvation. Believing in Him as God, our Creator as we are instructed in Scriptures is central to salvation. This is the most important step to consider in the discussions and views on Christ's Deity. In these discussions, it is always important to consider the Scriptures

Several other passages in the Scriptures give us significant indication about the Lord Jesus Christ as we read in the following paragraphs:

- *In Him, dwells the fullness of Deity:*

  [Col. 2:9], "For in Him all the fullness of Deity dwells in bodily form."

Equally important is that in our discussions about Christ's Deity, it should be clarified that Scriptures teach us that there is Only One God as we read in the Book of Isaiah:

I am the LORD, and there is no other;
apart from me there is no God [Isaiah 45:5].

Now, let us examine various headings with Scriptural description of the Lord Jesus Christ as God in the Flesh, God Who Is Worshiped, and God Who Is prayed to.

- *The Lord Jesus is God in the Flesh:*

The question to ask is: Was the Lord Jesus Christ truly God in the Flesh? To answer this question, we need to consider the Scriptures. The Lord Jesus Christ was God in in the Flesh because He was born of the Virgin by the power of the Holy Spirit as we read in the Book of Mathew: 1:21].

Moreover, the following passages instruct us that the Lord Jesus Christ was God in the Flesh:

- John 1:1, "In the beginning was the Word, and the Word was with God, and the Word was God."
- John 1:14, "And the Word became flesh, and dwelt among us, and we beheld His glory, glory as of the only begotten from the Father, full of grace and truth."
- "Thomas answered and said to Him, "My Lord and my God!" [John 20:28]
- Col. 2:9, "For in Him all the fullness of Deity dwells in bodily form."
- Phil. 2:5-8, "Have this attitude in yourselves which was also in Christ Jesus, 6 who, although He existed in *the form of God,* did not regard equality with God a thing to be grasped, 7 but emptied Himself, taking the form of a bond-servant, and being made in the likeness of men. 8 And being found in appearance as a man, He humbled Himself by becoming obedient to the point of death, even death on a cross. 9 Therefore also God highly exalted Him, and bestowed on Him the name which is above every name, 10 that at the name of Jesus every knee should bow, of those who are in heaven, and on earth, and under the earth, 11 and that every tongue should confess that Jesus Christ is Lord, to the glory of God the Father."

- "But of the Son He says, "*Thy throne, O God,* is forever and ever, and the righteous scepter is the scepter of His kingdom." [Heb. 1:8]
- And again, when God brings his firstborn into the world, he says, "Let all God's angels worship him." [Hebrews 1:6].
- "Thy throne, O God, is forever and ever; a scepter of uprightness is the scepter of Thy kingdom." Quoted from Psalm 45:6,
- But about the Son he says,
- "*Your throne, O God,* will last for ever and ever; a scepter of justice will be the scepter of your kingdom [Heb. 1:8]

Your throne, O God,[c] will last for ever and ever;
a scepter of justice will be the scepter of your kingdom.

The Lord Jesus Christ, God Who Is Worshiped

Scriptures are the inspired Word of God, and they inform us that the Lord Jesus Christ IS God Who Is worshipped. The Lord Jesus Christ Himself taught that God is the ONLY ONE to be worshipped; yet He receives worship. Yes, the Lord accepts to be worshipped, which teaches us that the Lord Jesus Christ is God, our Creator. The fact that the Lord Jesus Christ received worship indicates that He is God, our Creator. Let us examine a few passages where the Lord received worship. Please consider the following passages from Scriptures:

- Matt. 4:10, "Then Jesus said to him, 'Begone, Satan! For it is written, "***You shall worship the Lord your God, and serve Him only.***""""
- Matt. 2:2, "Where is He who has been born King of the Jews? For we saw His star in the east, and have come to worship Him."
- Matt. 2:11, "And they came into the house and saw the Child with Mary His mother; and they fell down and worshiped Him; and opening their treasures they presented to Him gifts of gold and frankincense and myrrh."
- Matt. 14:33, ***"And those who were in the boat worshiped Him,*** saying, "You are certainly God's Son!"
- Matt. 28:9, "And behold, Jesus met them and greeted them. And they came up and took hold of His feet ***and worshiped Him."***
- John 9:35-38, "Jesus heard that they had put him out; and finding him, He said, "Do you believe in the Son of Man?" 36 He answered

and said, "And who is He, Lord, that I may believe in Him?" 37 Jesus said to him, "You have both seen Him, and He is the one who is talking with you." 38 And he said, "Lord, I believe." **And he worshiped Him."**

- Heb. 1:6, "And when He again brings the first-born into the world, He says, 'And ***let all the angels of God worship Him.'"***

Obviously, the above passages that come from the Scriptures confirm to us that the Lord Jesus Christ received worship, this leads us to rightly conclude that the Lord Jesus Christ is God, Our Creator, because He said that Only God Is to be worshipped.

A glance at the attributes of God that include Omniscience, Omnipresence, and Holiness reveals that all these attributes apply to the nature of Our Lord Jesus Christ. Consider for example the Omniscience nature of God. Scriptures teach us that God knows everything including the thoughts in our hearts. Such knowledge God has been displaying is amazing. Those who are familiar with the Scriptures will recall that in the Book of Samuel I, in the Old Testament there is a remarkable incident, when the Lord God was looking for a King, and people chose Saul while the Lord God had chosen David. The lesson to learn here is obvious. We are instructed that God looks in the heart while men look at the external appearance.

In the Old Testament, in the Book of Psalm 139, we read that God perceives our thoughts from afar. Such knowledge reveals that God created us indeed and He made us in His image [Genesis 1:27]. God sees everything and He knows everything. Nothing in the world is hidden from God's sight. Even when Adam and Eve sinned and sought to run from God's sights, the Lord God saw everything and He knew everything. The fact that God knows everything and He sees everything encourages me personally for many reasons. First, it gives me peace and helps me to trust God. As I often share the painful experience of the tragedy that hit my family when my beloved brother André Tshibamba was kidnapped in the middle of the night and brutally murdered by the people he did not know, a tragedy I often remember with pain and tears, Only the Lord could assist me. I have learned to trust God for peace and for everything, and the thought that God knows everything and He sees everything helps me to have peace. Moreover, when Scriptures teach us that to God is the vengeance, one can but have peace and trust the Lord. God sees everything and God knows everything.

When you read about the Fall of Man in the book of Genesis Chapter 3, you realize that God knew well what happened and although He asked Adam: "Adam where are you?" He knew where Adam was and He knew what had happened and why Adam and Eve were seeking to hide from HIM. These incidents occurred and we read about them in the Old Testament and they teach us about the OMNISCIENCE Nature of God, as God knows and sees everything. Keeping this in mind, let us now examine the deeds of the Lord Jesus Christ during His earthly ministry as they also teach us much about His Omniscience Nature.

When you read Scriptures in the New Testament, you will realize that the Lord Jesus Christ knew the thoughts in peoples' hearts as we read in such passages as Matthew 9:4: "Knowing their thoughts, Jesus said, "Why do you entertain evil thoughts in your hearts?" This is one of the amazing facts that leaves one speechless. Who can know one's thoughts but God Himself?

Elsewhere in the same Book of Matthew, the Lord showed His Omniscience Nature by exposing their hidden thoughts: "Jesus knew their thoughts and said to them, "Every kingdom divided against itself will be ruined, and every city or household divided against itself will not stand "[Matthew 12:25]. Clearly, these examples confirm the omniscient nature of the Lord Jesus Christ and confirm that the Lord Jesus Christ is God, our Creator. The Omniscience attribute of God should make one ponder and fear HIM.

The omniscience nature of God is one of God's attributes that scares me and goes beyond my understanding because the awareness of the Omniscience Nature of God makes me aware that God knows me, He sees me and He knows my thoughts. If I do something with bad intentions, God sees it. For example, if I give someone a gift with the intention to mock a poor, God sees that I am mocking the poor. When you give to a poor, you lend to God and you honor God. "Whoever oppresses the poor shows contempt for their Maker, but whoever is kind to the needy honors God." Proverbs 19:17.

When I want to give a gift, I do it with delight. I know that God sees in my heart and my gift to the person will honor God and I am blessed. Scriptures teach us that "there is more joy in giving than in receiving." "God loves cheerful giver." And "He who gives to the poor lends to God."

When we do things with bad motives, we do not honor God. The Omniscient God is the Lord Jesus Christ! Things that are given to someone with bad intentions do not bring blessings. Many people would agree that things done with bad intentions have no benefits. Now, imagine when you know that God who created you sees everything you do, you should automatically change your intentions to honor God.

Another example of why we should be concerned and scared about the omniscient nature of God is that He sees everything and hears everything. Therefore, when you lie to a parent, a friend, or to your boss, the Lord hears all and knows your heart. When you think that God is omniscient and that He knows our thoughts and He sees them, you will realize that telling the truth is advantageous than lying because one lie leads to another; before you know it you become a liar which can cause more damage to you, to others, and to the community. When you tell the truth, you can ask for forgiveness, and the matter can be settled peacefully within your family, at work or in a relationship. Take for example a case of a relationship which is based on lies, when a man lies to his parents, his friends, to his fiancée or to his wife, those lies will cause the person who is lied to, to mistrust the man because of his lies. There will be dishonesty and lack of truth in the relationship which will lead to a broken or dysfunctional relationship and eventually to the separation. This is how men were separated from God and we needed the Savior and God became Man to save us [Genesis 3: 1-19; John 1:1-14]. We must remember that a lie brought on the Fall of Man. The Lord God told Adam and Eve not to eat from the forbidden fruit because on the day they did, they would die. But Satan lied to Eve and told her "You will surely not die." The consequence of this lie was the Fall of Man and God became Man to save the world [John 1:1-5]. Who do you think could save this world and repair the broken relationship between men and God, if not God Himself? No one else could save us but God Himself, Our Creator, the One Who created us, and the One Who loves us. God took on Flesh and came to us to earth to save us. He is the Lord Jesus Christ, our Creator as we read in the Book of [John 1-14]. Also, in the Book of Colossians [1:12-22]

[12] Giving thanks unto the Father, which hath made us meet to be partakers of the inheritance of the saints in light:

[13] Who hath delivered us from the power of darkness, and hath translated us into the kingdom of his dear Son:

[14] In whom we have redemption through his blood, even the forgiveness of sins:

[15] Who is the image of the invisible God, the firstborn of every creature:

[16] For by him were all things created, that are in heaven, and that are in earth, visible and invisible, whether they be thrones, or dominions, or principalities, or powers: all things were created by him, and for him:

[17] And he is before all things, and by him all things consist.

[18] And he is the head of the body, the church: who is the beginning, the firstborn from the dead; that in all things he might have the preeminence.

[19] For it pleased the Father that in him should all fulness dwell;

[20] And, having made peace through the blood of his cross, by him to reconcile all things unto himself; by him, I say, whether they be things in earth, or things in heaven.

[21] And you, that were sometime alienated and enemies in your mind by wicked works, yet now hath he reconciled

[22] In the body of his flesh through death, to present you holy and unblameable and unreproveable in his sight:

Colossians 1:12-22] KJV

Moreover, the Lord Jesus Christ is prayed to!

The Lord Jesus Christ Is Prayed to

Honestly, we all know that we can pray only to God, but how is it that Scriptures carry passages that show that the Lord Jesus Christ is prayed to? We can consider a few passages from the Scriptures that include the following:

- "But being full of the Holy Spirit, he gazed intently into heaven and saw the glory of God, and Jesus standing at the right hand of God; 56 and he said, "Behold, I see the heavens opened up and the Son of Man standing at the right hand of God." 57 But they cried out with a loud voice, and covered their ears, and they rushed upon him with one impulse. 58 And when they had driven him out of the city, they began stoning him, and the witnesses laid aside their robes at the feet of a young man named Saul. 59 And they went on stoning Stephen as he called upon the Lord and said, "Lord Jesus, receive my spirit!" 60 And falling on his knees, he cried out with a loud voice, "Lord, do not hold this sin against them!" And having said this, he fell asleep" [Acts 7:55-60].

Now, frankly speaking, a closer examination of the above passages from the Scriptures reveals a lot about the Deity of the Lord Jesus Christ and His Sovereignty, as He is prayed to. When the Lord Jesus Christ opened Stephen's eyes spiritually, to see HIM as Stephen was about to leave the earthly life, Stephens saw the Lord Jesus Christ in His glory, and he saw magnificence things that people who were around him and those who were stoning him could not see. Most people who have seen the visions and the dreams that are related to spirituality and heavenly things have testified to the Deity, the Sovereignty, and the Power of Our Lord and Savior Jesus Christ as the King of kings and the Lord of lords, the Almighty! Just read the Book of Revelation and note how the Lord reveals Himself in His glory as the King of kings, the Lord of lords, the Judge, and the Word of God, the Almighty God!

- "Paul, called as an apostle of Jesus Christ by the will of God, and Sosthenes our brother, 2 to the church of God which is at Corinth, to those who have been sanctified in Christ Jesus, saints by calling, with all who in every place call upon the name of our Lord Jesus Christ, their Lord and ours" [1 Cor. 1:1-2].

In the passages above, we can notice that Paul asks Christians at the Church in Corinth to call upon the Lord Jesus Christ. To call upon the Lord means to pray to the Lord, as most believers would agree.

Moreover, it is important to remember that to call upon the Lord means to pray to Him, as we read in following passages in the Old Testament.

- "Then you call on the name of your god, and I ***will call on the name of the Lord, and the God who answers by fire, He is God.*** " And all the people answered and said, "That is a good idea." [1 Kings 18:24]
- "And I will bring the third part through the fire, refine them as silver is refined, and test them as gold is tested. They will call on My name, and I will answer them; I will say, 'They are My people,' and they will say, 'The Lord is my God.'" [Zech. 13:9].
- "for 'whoever ***will call upon*** the name of the Lord' will be saved." 14 How then shall they call upon Him in whom they have not believed? And how shall they believe in Him whom they have not heard?" [Rom. 10:13-14]
- "And it shall come to pass, that whosoever ***shall call on the name of the LORD shall be delivered***: for in Mount Zion and in Jerusalem shall be deliverance, as the LORD hath said, and in the remnant whom the LORD shall call." [Joel 2:32]. (LORD here is YHWH, the name of God as revealed in Exodus 3:14.

In other versions we read:

- And everyone who calls
   on the name of the LORD will be saved;
for on Mount Zion and in Jerusalem
   there will be deliverance,
   as the LORD has said,
even among the survivors
   whom the LORD calls [Joel 2:32]. NIV

Therefore, the Lord Jesus Christ is God, Our Creator because these quotes that deal with God Himself are attributed to the Lord Jesus Christ.

Only God can be prayed to. To pray to God can mean adoring HIM, imploring, praising Him, and worshipping HIM. When we pray to God, we recognize our state of sinful nature, our weaknesses, and our desperate need for the Lord, for part from HIM, we cannot do anything.

- **The First and The Last**

To be the First and the Last, is one of the most challenging passages and yet it is very clear because only God is the First and the Last. Because Our lord and Savior Jesus Christ is the First and the Last, He Must be God, Our Creator.

- Isaiah 44:6, "Thus says the Lord, the King of Israel and his Redeemer, the Lord of hosts: 'I am the first and I am the last, and there is no God besides Me."
- Rev. 1:17-18, "Do not be afraid; I am the first and the last, 18 and the living One; and I was dead, and behold, I am alive forevermore, and I have the keys of death and of Hades."

These passages from the Scriptures clearly indicate to us that the Lord Jesus Christ is God, our Creator. Unless one really does not want to believe in God or refuses to seek His assistance to know that the Lord Jesus Christ Is God, Our Creator will he or she miss the truth that there is Only One God, the Lord Jesus Christ, Our Creator. When one fails to seek assistance, one will miss to see that God exits, He Is One and He can functions as the Father, The Son and The Holy Spirit.

Conclusion

The nature of the Lord Jesus Christ clearly tells us that the Lord Is God, Our Creator. Many indicators including His names, His titles, and His attributes reveal to us that the Lord Jesus Christ IS God, Our Creator. For example, Scriptures teach that the name Immanuel means "God with us" as we read: "The virgin will conceive and give birth to a son, and they will call him Immanuel" (which means "God with us") [Matthew 1:23].

Also, the Lord's name Jesus means the Savior as we read in Scriptures: "She will give birth to a son, and you are to give him the name Jesus, because he will save his people from their sins." [Matthew 1:21].

Activities for the chapter

1. Which verses from the Scriptures teach us that the Lord Jesus Christ has never sinned?

    ____
    ____
    ____
    ____

2. Do you think that a sinner could redeem the world from the curse?

    ____
    ____
    ____
    ____

3. Write down Biblical passage (s) that teach us that Only the Spotless Lamb could redeem the world and be Our Savior.

    ____
    ____
    ____
    ____

4. Write down passages from the Scriptures that refer to the Lord Jesus as LORD of all.

    ____
    ____
    ____
    ____

CHAPTER 5

The Lord Jesus Christ's Claim about HIMSELF

> "Very truly I tell you," Jesus answered, "before Abraham was born, I am!" [John 8:58].

The identity of an individual is critical and matters a great deal. In most societies, people will seek to know about people around them, those at work and those they associate with. This curiosity often pushes company to investigate people before they hire them. Similarly, this curiosity causes most individuals to conduct research about other people prior to socializing with them. In most societies prior to getting engaged in a serious relationship, there is a need to seek to know an individual. Similarly, prior to hiring a new employee, the supervisor or the manager seeks to know the person they will hire. More often, they also ask the individual to tell who they say they are.

In most cases, people will send a resume along with cover letters for a given position. In addition, they will send letters of recommendations. Now, notice that more often during the interview, the employer often asks the applicants to tell them who they are. They would like to hear from the applicants themselves about who they say they are. Therefore, the statement: "tell us about yourself."

In the case of the Lord Jesus Christ, we know that the Scriptures in the Holy Bible give us His resume or the Curriculum Vitae (CV). For example, we read about the Genealogy of Christ in the four books of the New Testament.

His disciples also tell us who Jesus is. For example, Peter tells us that the Lord Jesus Christ is the Messiah, the anointed One [Matthew 16:16]. As for John, he said that the Lord Jesus Christ is the Eternal God [John 1:2]. In Hebrews 1:18-12], we read that the Lord Jesus Christ Is Eternal God.

Other people also testify about Jesus.

The apostle Paul declares that Christ is the visible image of the invisible God in the Book of Colossians. For his part the evangelist, John declares that Jesus Christ existed in the beginning with God, He is the Word of God and He is God as we read in the Book of John.

And Peter teaches us that: "you must worship Christ as Lord of your life."

But mostly, it is important to know who the Lord Jesus claims HE IS.

In the following paragraphs, we will read about Jesus' Claims about Himself. Did the Lord Jesus ever say that he is God?

The Lord Jesus Himself declared that He Is before Abraham was.

> "Very truly I tell you," Jesus answered, "before Abraham was born, I am!" [John 8:58].

To well know someone, you need to know who he said He Is.

The Lord Jesus made the following statements:

- The Lord said that He Is before Abraham was.

  "Your father Abraham rejoiced as he looked forward to my coming. He saw it and was glad."

  The people said, "You aren't even fifty years old. How can you say you have seen Abraham?"

  Jesus answered, "I tell you the truth, before Abraham was even born, I Am!"[4]

- The Lord Jesus said that He and the Father are one [John 30:10].
- Jesus said that He who sees Him, has seen the Father

  Philip said, "Lord, show us the Father, and we will be satisfied."

  Jesus replied, "Have I been with you all this time, Philip, and yet you still don't know who I am? Anyone who has seen me has seen the Father! So why are you asking me to show him to you?"

- Jesus said that He has the power to forgive Sins:

  "...that you may know that the Son of Man has authority on earth to forgive sins"--he then said to the paralytic--"Rise, pick up your bed and go home." And he rose and went home. When the crowds saw it, they were afraid, and they glorified God..."[7]

  He said to them, "You are from below; I am from above. You are of this world; I am not of this world. I told you that you would die in your sins, for unless you believe that I am he you will die in your sins."[8]

Jesus said that He is the judge and He gives Eternal Life.

- "For as the Father raises the dead and gives them life, so also the Son gives life to whom he will. The Father judges no one, but has given all judgment to the Son, that all may honor the Son, just as they honor the Father."[9]
- Jesus said to her, "I am the resurrection and the life. Whoever believes in me, though he die, yet shall he live."[10]
- "My sheep hear my voice, and I know them, and they follow me. I give them eternal life, and they will never perish, and no one will snatch them out of my hand."[11]
- "For it is my Father's will that all who see his Son and believe in him should have eternal life. I will raise them up at the last day."[12]
- Jesus said that He is the Source of Life
- Jesus said He is the same as the Father

"The Father and I are one."

Once again, the people picked up stones to kill him.

Jesus said, "At my Father's direction I have done many good works. For which one are you going to stone me?"

They replied, "We're stoning you not for any good work, but for blasphemy! You, a mere man, claim to be God."

- The Lord said: No one knows the father
- Jesus shouted to the crowds, "If you trust me, you are trusting not only me, but also God who sent me. For when you see me, you are seeing the one who sent me. I have come as a light to shine in this dark world, so that all who put their trust in me will no longer remain in the dark."[5]

No one goes to the Father except through Him.

- "No one can come to the Father except through me. If you had really known me, you would know who my Father is. From now on, you do know him and have seen him!"
- Philip said, "Lord, show us the Father, and we will be satisfied."
- Jesus replied, "Have I been with you all this time, Philip, and yet you still don't know who I am? Anyone who has seen me has seen the Father! So why are you asking me to show him to you?"[6]
- *Jesus Said He Existed Before Abraham*
- "Your father Abraham rejoiced as he looked forward to my coming. He saw it and was glad."
- The people said, "You aren't even fifty years old. How can you say you have seen Abraham?"
- Jesus answered, "I tell you the truth, before Abraham was even born, I Am!"[4]

Jesus Said to See Him is the Same as Seeing God

- Jesus shouted to the crowds, "If you trust me, you are trusting not only me, but also God who sent me. For when you see me, you are seeing the one who sent me. I have come as a light to shine in this dark world, so that all who put their trust in me will no longer remain in the dark."[5]

- "No one can come to the Father except through me. If you had really known me, you would know who my Father is. From now on, you do know him and have seen him!"
- Philip said, "Lord, show us the Father, and we will be satisfied."
- Jesus replied, "Have I been with you all this time, Philip, and yet you still don't know who I am? Anyone who has seen me has seen the Father! So why are you asking me to show him to you?"[6]

Jesus Said He Could Forgive Sins

- "...that you may know that the Son of Man has authority on earth to forgive sins"--he then said to the paralytic--"Rise, pick up your bed and go home." And he rose and went home. When the crowds saw it, they were afraid, and they glorified God..."[7]
- He said to them, "You are from below; I am from above. You are of this world; I am not of this world. I told you that you would die in your sins, for unless you believe that I am he you will die in your sins."[8]

Jesus Said He Is the Judge and Can Grant Eternal Life

> "For as the Father raises the dead and gives them life, so also the Son gives life to whom he will. The Father judges no one, but has given all judgment to the Son, that all may honor the Son, just as they honor the Father."[9]
>
> Jesus said to her, "I am the resurrection and the life. Whoever believes in me, though he die, yet shall he live."[10]
>
> "My sheep hear my voice, and I know them, and they follow me. I give them eternal life, and they will never perish, and no one will snatch them out of my hand."[11]
>
> "For it is my Father's will that all who see his Son and believe in him should have eternal life. I will raise them up at the last day."[12]

Jesus Said He Was the Same as God

- "The Father and I are one."
- Once again the people picked up stones to kill him.
- Jesus said, "At my Father's direction I have done many good works. For which one are you going to stone me?"
- They replied, "We're stoning you not for any good work, but for blasphemy! You, a mere man, claim to be God."[13]

Jesus Said He Is Our Source for Life.

"I Am the Bread of Life"

Jesus replied, "I am the bread of life. Whoever comes to me will never be hungry again. Whoever believes in me will never be thirsty."[14]

"I am the way, the truth, the life"

Jesus said to him, "I am the way, the truth, and the life. No one can come to the Father except through me."[15]

"I am the Light of the world"

"I am the light of the world. Whoever follows me will not walk in darkness, but will have the light of life."[16]

"you will know the truth"

"If you abide in my word, you are truly my disciples, and you will know the truth, and the truth will set you free."[17]

"have life, abundantly"

The Lord Jesus Christ Is Life, He gives Life in Abundance, He is the Author of Life.

Conclusion

The Lord Jesus Christ is God in the Flesh, He is our Creator indeed. Scriptures teach us about our Creator and the works He accomplished when He visited us on earth. The works that the Lord Jesus Christ accomplished on earth testify to His Deity and to the fact that He is God, our Creator.

Activities for this chapter

1. Who is the Source of Life according to Scriptures in the Holy Bible?

 ____

 ____

 ____

 ____

2. Who do you think gives life to human beings?

 ____

 ____

 ____

 ____

CHAPTER 6

The Most Difficult Thing to Comprehend

> The Word became flesh and made his dwelling among us. We have seen his glory, the glory of the one and only Son, who came from the Father, full of grace and truth.
>
> [15] (John testified concerning him. He cried out, saying, "This is the one I spoke about when I said, 'He who comes after me has surpassed me because he was before me.'") [16] Out of his fullness we have all received grace in place of grace already given. [17] For the law was given through Moses; grace and truth came through Jesus Christ. [18] No one has ever seen God, but the one and only Son, who is himself God and[b] is in closest relationship with the Father, has made him known [John 1:14-18].

The most difficult thing for many to believe is that God took on Flesh and became Man. Even though it is clearly stated in the Scriptures that God became Man, as one can clearly see from the passage above, some people still doubt the Word of God. Most people agree that the Lord Jesus Christ lived on earth, but they do not accept that He is God. The life of the Lord Jesus Christ on earth does not seem to present more challenges to minds because most historical records testify to the Lord's life on earth. His teachings, His crucifixion, and His resurrection have been recorded in historical records by scholars who believe in the Scriptures and scholars who even reject the truth of the Holy Bible.

There are many challenging historical events that many historians do disagree upon and question all the time, please be assured that the life of Our Lord and Savior Jesus Christ on earth is not one of them. If you remove the life of the Lord Jesus Christ on earth and His earthly ministry, history will not make sense. Most scholars including historians and archaeologists agree on the fact that the Lord Jesus Christ lived on earth and many religious scholars including reverend Matt Slick, as well as scholars who have written about World History have elaborated on this topic. One can read about the historical evidence of the life of the Lord Jesus Christ on earth by various scholars, among them religious and none religious scholars.

The life of the Lord Jesus Christ on earth is not one of them because historical evidence has testified to the life of the Lord Jesus Christ on earth. For example, the archaeological evidence in the tomb where The Body of the Lord Jesus Christ was laid and evidence of His teachings and the records of the works of His disciples have been found.

Historical factors are often related in major historical books, in written literature and even in oral literature. In the case of Christianity and the accounts of theological factors and events, most scholars believe that the Holy Bible has recorded significant issues related to creation, historical events and the life of Jesus Christ. In fact most historians have made statements that the name of The Lord Jesus Christ refers to a character who existed and who lived on earth at a certain period of time and He has marked World History. His life presented challenges more than any other character who has ever lived. Therefore, the birth and the crucifixion of The Lord Jesus Christ have been recorded in most historical texts as we read such references as: *Before Christ (BC*) and *After Christ AD*. Some people may also refer to CE (the Common Era), but in most historical books references often used the landmarks, *Before Christ or After Christ*. These references are used not only in English, but also in many other classical and ordinary languages. Scholars have used the term BC and AC to relate major historical events in World History. For example, in the French language, there is always the references, A*vant la Naissance de Jesus Christ ou après,* la naissance de Jesus Christ. These facts confirm the presence of the Lord Jesus Christ on earth at a certain period of time and therefore establish the fact of His existence.

Now, the presence of the Lord Jesus Christ on earth does not seem to challenge many people, rather it is His nature, and His claims. Mostly, it is the Lord's claim about WHO He says that He IS that causes challenges to many people during the time of His earthly ministry and even after He ascended to heaven. The doubt has lingered in some people's minds throughout history and even today. A glance at the Scriptures, the inspired Word of God reveals that the nature of our Lord Jesus Christ and the mighty works that He accomplished including healing the sick, forgiving sins and raising people from death have pushed many to even ask the Lord to tell them Who HE says He IS and the LORD told them who He IS, and the answers even troubled many more as we read in such passages as: "If you are the Messiah," they said, "tell us." Jesus answered, "If I tell you, you will not believe me,.. [22:67].

Interestingly enough is the fact that even His disciples had trouble to figure out Who the LORD Jesus Christ IS.

At one point the Lord Himself asked the disciples to tell Him Who they say He IS: "But what about you?" he asked. "Who do you say I am?" Peter answered, "You are the Messiah." [Mark 8:29].

Who do you say I AM?

To this question, Peter answered: "You are the Messiah." .... And the Lord said that my Father reveals this to you. One would think that this discussion solved the issue about Who the Lord Jesus Christ IS, and that all His disciples would agree to everything He had told them. But after Our Lord and Savior Jesus Christ offered Himself as RANSOM, went to the Cross to be crucified to give us salvation, and He rose from the dead after three days, Scriptures recall another remarkable moment of doubt when one of the Lord's disciples doubted the fact that the Lord Jesus had risen from the dead. Scriptures recall the story of Thomas who doubted the Lord's resurrection, but ultimately fell at the Lord's feet and made a powerful statement, *"My Lord and My God."*

My Lord and My God."

Clearly, this statement shows that Thomas, recognized Christ's Deity and admitted that the LORD Jesus Christ is God, Our Creator. There is only One God, WHO Is the Creator and who created the Heavens and the Earth. If Thomas admitted and recognized the LORD Jesus as His

Creator, the Creator of the Universe, what does this recognition mean to all God's creatures?

There are few points that I have mentioned in the paragraphs above including the Nature of the Lord Jesus Christ, His earthly ministry, and the challenging question He asked His disciples to say "WHO they say He IS?" I also mentioned Peter's answer to the Lord Jesus's question as He answered by stating that the Lord Jesus Christ is the Messiah. I will elaborate more on these subjects in the following paragraphs. In addition, we will discuss the powerful statement Thomas, made when he fell at the Lord's Feet and stated: "My Lord and My God."

Scriptures, the inspired Word of God instruct us that Thomas fell at the Lord's feet. Clearly we can say that Thomas worshipped the Lord Jesus Christ after the Lord rose from death. Then the question we can ask is: Why did Thomas Worship the LORD Jesus Christ if Jesus Christ Is Not God as Scriptures teach that Only God Is to be worshipped? Even more interesting question is: Why did the Lord Jesus Christ accept worship from the Thomas and other peoples as we read in other passages of the Scriptures? Thomas fell at the feet of the Lord Jesus Christ and stated: MY LORD and My God! This is a critical historical event that must be considered in the discussions about Christ's Deity because it provides us with evidence that the Lord Jesus Christ is God, Our Creator just as other statements in John Isaiah 9:6; John 1:1-15, Colossians 1:15-20 and Hebrews chapter 1:6 to mention these.

Although historians have informed us about the presence of the Lord Jesus Christ on earth and His remarkable earthly ministry, and Scriptures teach us Christ's Deity, there are still many people who challenge the truth about Christ's Deity. One of the reasons is that as human beings, we cannot comprehend that God, our Creator, the Creator of the Universe took on flesh to become Man and to live among men. It is hard to think that God Our Creator decided to become like us and form a Body to dwell in. This thought alone can be challenging for us to comprehend that God can became Man. He lived among men and went to the Cross, gave Himself as the Sacrifice on His own accord to redeem us. This is what many of us cannot comprehend Unless God Himself assists us to believe in Him and in His Word.

To face the most difficult challenge, we need to pray to God for assistance. We need to read the word of God and search for answers in His Word because His Word IS Truth.

I believe that Christ's Deity is the most challenging question for all men and women because it is difficult for most people to comprehend that God took on flesh and became Man to dwell among the people He created; this is the most difficult challenge because Only God can help us to understand and believe in this powerful truth.

> Peter Declares That Jesus Is the Messiah
>
> [13] When Jesus came to the region of Caesarea Philippi, he asked his disciples, "Who do people say the Son of Man is?"
>
> [14] They replied, "Some say John the Baptist; others say Elijah; and still others, Jeremiah or one of the prophets."
>
> [15] "But what about you?" he asked. "Who do you say I am?"
>
> [16] Simon Peter answered, "You are the Messiah, the Son of the living God."
>
> [17] Jesus replied, "Blessed are you, Simon son of Jonah, for this was not revealed to you by flesh and blood, *but by my Father in heaven.* [18] And I tell you that you are Peter,[b] and on this rock I will build my church, and the gates of Hades[c] will not overcome it. [19] I will give you the keys of the kingdom of heaven; whatever you bind on earth will be[d] bound in heaven, and whatever you loose on earth will be[e] loosed in heaven." [20] Then he ordered his disciples not to tell anyone that he was the Messiah [Matthew 16:15].

Scriptures show clearly that the Lord Jesus Christ is God, our Creator.

For examples, the following Bible verses show that the Lord Jesus Christ is Divine. For examples these verses instruct us that, the Lord Jesus Christ is God in Flesh, He is worshipped and He is prayed to as we read:

1. The Lord Jesus is God in Flesh. We can read this information in the following verses.

    - John 1:1, "In the beginning was the Word, and the Word was with God, and the Word was God."

Scriptures teach that The Lord Jesus Christ is the First and the Last

- Isaiah 44:6, "Thus says the Lord, the King of Israel and his Redeemer, the Lord of hosts: 'I am the first and I am the last, and there is no God besides Me."
- Rev. 1:17-18, "Do not be afraid; I am the first and the last, 18 and the living One; and I was dead, and behold, I am alive forevermore, and I have the keys of death and of Hades."
- Scriptures also teach that the Lord Jesus Christ is worshipped
- While [Jesus] spake these things unto them, behold, there came a certain ruler, and worshipped him... Matthew 9:18

Only God is worshipped.	Jesus is worshipped.
... Then saith Jesus unto him... Thou shalt worship the Lord thy God, and him only shalt thou serve. Matthew 4:10	While [Jesus] spake these things unto them, behold, there came a certain ruler, and worshipped him... Matthew 9:18 And again, when [God] bringeth in the first begotten [Jesus] into the world, he saith, And let all the angels of God worship him. Hebrews 1:6 And Thomas answered and said unto [Jesus], My Lord and my God. John 20:28

Conclusion

As Scriptures teach that the Lord Jesus Christ is God, Our Creator, we must believe this for God does not lie. Moreover, without faith, it is impossible to please Him.

Activities for this chapter

1. Write down few Biblical verses that teach us about God's existence and underline the verses that state that there is only One God.

   ____
   ____
   ____
   ____

2. Which of the verses you read about God's existence are convincing and inspiring in your opinion?

   ____
   ____
   ____
   ____

3. Indicate the verses that present challenges and present them to God and ask for clarity or revelation.

   ____
   ____
   ____
   ____

CHAPTER 7

A Conversation with Jesus

> Greater love has no one than this: to lay down one's life for one's friends. [John 15:13].

The Lord Jesus Christ calls us His friends and He came to earth to save us. The Lord's friendship with us is unique because He gives more to His friends. The Lord has given us so much, even to the point of leaving His glory to give us life. Friendship brings blessings. When you have the Lord Jesus Christ as your friend, you will receive many blessings and above all, the Lord gives salvation and eternal life as He said. "I give them eternal life, and they shall never perish; no one will snatch them out of my hand." This is a blessing worthy receiving. Elsewhere, the Lord explains that there is no greater love than this: There is no greater love than to lay down one's life for one's friends [John13:15].

Imagine having a conversation with the Lord Jesus and He asks you to be His friend and He gives you many reasons to become His friend such as the forgiveness of sins, giving you peace, salvation and eternal life. The Lord tells you, "I love you, I gave my life for you, I will forgive your sins. The Lord continues and says: "I will give you peace, and I will give you eternal life. Bring your burden to me, I will give you a lighter load: 'For my yoke is easy and my burden is light' [Matthew 11:30]. The Lord gives peace. Above all, He gives eternal life; receiving eternal life means to know Him [John17:3]. What reason do you give to reject His friendship?

Despite our disobedience, God shows us His amazing love, grace and mercy for while we were still sinners, He loved us and He died for us,

> While we were still sinners, Christ died for us [Romans 5:8].

He came to earth to save us. The Lord says that He is the Way, the Truth and the Life. We read this in John 14:6. This passage teaches us about the Deity of Our Lord and Savior Lord Jesus Christ and confirms that the Lord Jesus IS God because Only God is the Savior as we read: "I, even I, am the LORD, and apart from me there is no savior." [Isaiah 43:11].

Imagine meeting the Lord Jesus Christ somewhere, in a dream, in the street or in the life hereafter, and He asks you; "Who do you think I AM"? What would you say? This is one of the questions to consider while we are still on earth.

Concerning the friendship and the love that Our Savior gives us, we need to love Him because we need Him. There are many reasons that encourage us to love the Lord including, His amazing love for us and the salvation He gives to whoever believes in Him. While there are many reasons that can cause one to love Our Lord and Savior, Jesus Christ, there is one reason that remains clear, that is that the Lord Jesus Christ is God, our Creator. The Lord created us and He breathed life in us. For this very reasons, one must feel the need to Love Him and to believe in Him.

As a matter of fact the Lord Jesus Christ took on flesh to come to earth to save us.

> In the beginning was the Word, *and the Word was with God, and the Word was God.* [2] He was with God in the beginning. [3] Through him all things were made; without him nothing was made that has been made. [4] In him was life, and that life was the light of all mankind. [5] The light shines in the darkness, and the darkness has not overcome[a] it.
>
> [6] There was a man sent from God whose name was John. [7] He came as a witness to testify concerning that light, so that through him all might believe. [8] He himself was not the light; he came only as a witness to the light.
>
> [9] The true light that gives light to everyone was coming into the world. [10] He was in the world, and though the world was made through him, the world did not recognize him. [11] He came to that which was his own, but his own did not receive him. [12] Yet to all

> who did receive him, to those who believed in his name, he gave the right to become children of God— [13] children born not of natural descent, nor of human decision or a husband's will, but born of God.
>
> [14] The Word became flesh and made his dwelling among us. We have seen his glory, the glory of the one and only Son, who came from the Father, full of grace and truth.
>
> [15] (John testified concerning him. He cried out, saying, "This is the one I spoke about when I said, 'He who comes after me has surpassed me because he was before me.'") [16] Out of his fullness we have all received grace in place of grace already given. [17] For the law was given through Moses; grace and truth came through Jesus Christ. [18] No one has ever seen God, but the one and only Son, *who is himself God* and[b] is in closest relationship with the Father, has made him known [John 1:1-18].

God so loves the world that He gave His one and only begotten Son, the Lord Jesus Christ came to save us.

Jesus Christ calls us His friend

The Lord Jesus Christ exists, He is Our Savior and He is the greatest Friend to have. No one can love us as the Lord loves us. There is no greater love than the love the Lord offers us. No one in this world can love us as the Lord loves us.

The Lord loves us, He created us in His images [Genesis 1:27]. Despite, man's disobedience and the fall of man, God became Man to save us.

This chapter raises a question, Who Is the Creator of the Universe?

There is Only One God, He came to earth to save us. He is our Lord and Savior Jesus Christ.

It is written that in the beginning was the Word and the Word was with God and the Word was Go[1:1-2]. This is a very powerful passage that shows us Who the Creator of the Universe Is.

Conclusion

It is always important to read Scriptures, to pray to God to ask that He opens our minds to understand His Word and His will. How can one possibly deny God's existence, when nature teaches us about God and declares His Glory! How can one resist to believe that the Lord Jesus Christ is God, our Creator when Scriptures teach us about Him and provide us with all the Lord's attributes. His works and His nature testify evidence to His Deity! Praying to God can help us to learn more about Who He Is, Immanuel, God with us [Matthew 1:23].

Imagine having a conversation with Jesus Christ.

Activities for this chapter

1. Scriptures teach that there is Only One God.

   Which passage (s) from the Scriptures ministers to you or convinces you the most about this powerful truth that there is Only ONE GOD?

   ____
   ____
   ____
   ____

2. Who do you say the Lord Jesus Christ Is?

   ____
   ____
   ____
   ____

CHAPTER 8

Who Do You Say I Am?

> "But what about you?" he asked. "Who do you say I a m?" [16] Simon Peter answered, "You are the Messiah, the Son of the living God." [Matthew 16: 15:16]

Imagine walking in the street and you start thinking, your thoughts got deeper and deeper, then suddenly, you start singing in a lower voice, and as you sang your voice got lower and lower, then, suddenly you fell asleep. While sleeping, you continue singing and thinking in your sleep, as your subconscious continues to process your thoughts while you are in your deep sleep you start dreaming, remembering your life and pondering about your life. As you are thinking, then stopping to sing and then back to thinking and singing again, unwillingly and unknowingly you suddenly find yourself in front of the seat of the judgement and you see the JUDGE sitting on the judgement seat. Then, you realize that He is not an ordinary judge you can argue with. In addition, you notice that He is the JUDGE and He IS also the LAWYER. As you think about claiming your rights or remaining silent, and calling a lawyer, He looks at you and somehow communicates to you that He can also be your lawyer. After a moment of silence, He asks you a challenging question: "WHO do you Say I AM? He asks you this question just as He asked His disciples during His earthly ministry. Peter called Him the Messiah as we read in the New Testament, and Thomas called Him LORD and God, how about you? Is the Lord Jesus Christ your LORD and Your God?

When the Lord appeared to Thomas after the resurrection, he stated: "My Lord and My God."

> [24] Now Thomas (also known as Didymium[a]), one of the Twelve, was not with the disciples when Jesus came. [25] So the other disciples told him, "We have seen the Lord!"
>
> But he said to them, "Unless I see the nail marks in his hands and put my finger where the nails were, and put my hand into his side, I will not believe."
>
> [26] A week later his disciples were in the house again, and Thomas was with them. Though the doors were locked, Jesus came and stood among them and said, "Peace be with you!" [27] Then he said to Thomas, "Put your finger here; see my hands. Reach out your hand and put it into my side. Stop doubting and believe."

[28] Thomas said to him, "My Lord and my God!"

[29] Then Jesus told him, "Because you have seen me, you have believed; blessed are those who have not seen and yet have believed" [John 24:29].

The Names of the Lord Jesus Christ reveal much and tell us about WHO He IS. And these names teach us that the Lord Jesus is God, our Creator.

There are more than 200 hundred names and titles that describe the Lord Jesus Christ in the Scriptures, the inspired Word of God. Although we know that this number is reduced, as other scholars have made mention of a larger number such as 700 names and tiles of the Lord Jesus, I will content myself to mention 200 names and titles of the Lord Jesus Christ. I urge the audience to take a look at these few names in the following paragraphs and make their own list to find out the truth. I sincerely believe that there are more than 200 names of the Lord and some of those include the Beginning and the End, Alpha and Omega, Eternal God, the Truth, and the Life.

In Scriptures the Lord Jesus Christ IS described as the:

> Chief Cornerstone: [Ephesians 2:20].
>
> Head of the Church: [Ephesians 1:22; 4:15; 5:23]

Holy One:

Judge: [Acts 10:42; 2 Timothy 4:8]

King of kings and Lord of lords: (1 Timothy 6:15; Revelation 19:16)

Light of the World: [John 8:12]

Prince of peace: [Isaiah 9:6]

Mighty God :

Son of God: [Luke 1:35; John 1:49]

Son of man: [John 5:27] .

Word: [John 1:1; 1 John 5:7-8]

Word of God: [Revelation 19:12-13]

Word of Life: [1 John 1:1]

The Lord Jesus Christ's Names and titles are powerful, they teach us that the Lord is God, our Creator. He gives us life, there is no other beside Him. Those names include the following:

Author of Life

Alpha and Omega: (Revelation 1:8; 22:13) – Jesus declared Himself to be the beginning and the end of all things, a reference to no one but the true God. This statement of everlasting nature could apply only to God.

Emmanuel: (Isaiah 9:6; Matthew 1:23) – Literally "God with us." Both Isaiah and Matthew affirm that the Christ who would be born in Bethlehem would be God Himself who came to earth in the form of a man to live among His people.

The I Am: (John 8:58, with Exodus 3:14) –

The Lord of All: (Acts 10:36) – Jesus is the sovereign ruler over the whole world and all things in it, of all the nations of the world, and particularly of the people of God's choosing, Gentiles as well as Jews.

The True God: (1 John 5:20) –

The True Vine: (John 15:1)

Eternal God:

Deuteronomy 33:
The eternal God is your refuge, and underneath are the everlasting arms. He will drive out your enemies before you, saying, 'Destroy them!'

Jesus Christ is the same yesterday and today and forever [Hebrews 13:8].

Truly, the Lord Jesus Christ Is Eternal.

Read the following passages from the Scriptures for yourself:

In John 10:28, Jesus said, *"And I give unto them eternal life; and they shall never perish, neither shall any man pluck them out of my hand."* If Jesus Christ isn't eternal, then how does He have the power to give "eternal life"?

Micah 5:2 states that Jesus Christ is "from everlasting", which is exactly what Psalm 93:2 and Isaiah 63:16 say about God!

In John 8:58, Jesus said to the Pharisees, "Verily, verily, I say unto you, Before Abraham was, I am." The term "I am" is the exact term that God used in Exodus 3:14 in reference to Himself! Jesus professed to be the eternal God of the Bible.

Also important is the meaning of His Names, the Lord Jesus Christ has Divine Names. For examples: The Lord Jesus Christ is called Immanuel, which means God with us. The Lord is also called Everlasting Father. All these names are discussed in the Scriptures as we read:

- In Matthew 22:42-45, Jesus claims to be the "Lord" in Psalm 110:1. He allows Thomas to address Him as "My Lord and my God" in John 20:28.
- He is the "everlasting Father" and "The mighty God" in Isaiah 9:6.
- According to His own words in John 10:11-14, He is the "shepherd." Also in Psalm 23:1, Psalm 80:1, and Ezekiel 34:12.
- God is the "savior" in Isaiah 43:3, 43:11, 45:15, 45:21, Hosea 13:4, Luke 1:47, and I Timothy 4:10, yet this same title is given to Jesus Christ in Luke 2:11, Philippians 3:20, II Timothy 1:10, and II Peter 2:20.
- God is the "Rock" in Deuteronomy 32:4, 32:15, 32:18, 32:30-31, I Samuel 2:2, and Psalm 18:31, yet this title is given to the Lord Jesus Christ in I Corinthians 10:1-4, I Peter 2:7-8, and Romans 9:33.

The effective way to learn about Christ's Deity is to examine the Scriptures with honesty, humility, and an open-mind. In addition, one needs to pray to the Lord for assistance. Read for yourself and examine the Scriptures. They are very clear about the One and Only God, the Savior of the World.

- God is "light" in Psalm 27:1 and Micah 7:8, and then Jesus is "light" in John 1:4-9 and in John 8:12.
- In Isaiah 44:6 God says, "...I *am* the first, and I *am* the last; and beside me *there is* no God." In Revelation 1:17 Jesus Christ says, "...Fear not; I am the first and the last."

  The Scriptures clearly show that the Lord Jesus Christ is the God of the Old Testament.

  Even when you read about the Lord's works and functions, you will notice that there are the works and functions of God, Our Creator. There is Only One God and He Is our Lord and Savior Jesus

Christ. For examples, Who can be the Ruler of God's Creation but God Himself! And Who can be the Rock, but God Himself!

The Ruler of God's Creation. In the Book of Revelation

Also the Rock. Who can be the Rock but God Himself!

The Rock: Psalm 18:2

Many verses instruct us about the Lord's ministry on earth and reveal that the Lord is Our Creator. Remarkable events such as raising the dead, accepting to be worshipped, accepting to be crucified to save His people, as well as His resurrection clearly instruct us that the Lord Jesus Christ is God, Our Creator.

Moreover, the Lord Jesus Christ raised Himself from death.

He raised Himself from the dead

Most people who believe in Scriptures recall that the Lord Jesus Christ talked about the crucifixion, and about His resurrection long before these events took place. Moreover, the Lord also indicated that He would raise Himself from the dead as we read:

Jesus answered them, "Destroy this temple, and I will raise it again in three days." [John2:19]

This clearly showed that the Lord Jesus Christ Is God, Our Creator, otherwise. Who can raise Himself and produce such wonders, but God Himself?

The Lord Is God indeed.

He was worshipped and He accepted to be worshipped. For examples, the magi worshipped the Lord.

Moreover, the Lord Jesus Christ is prayed to. According to the Scriptures, we are only to pray to God, not to anyone else. In the Books of Acts, we are told that Stephen, one of the stronger believers and followers of the Lord Jesus Christ, prayed to the Lord Jesus Christ, Now, why would Stephen prayed to the Lord, if He Was Not God, our Creator?.

The Lord is also called the Author of Life.

How can one be the author of life and not be God?!

It was Peter who made such a powerful statement. "You Killed the Author of Life"

Moreover, the Lord Jesus Christ is the Author of our faith.

The Lord gives life as He said. I came to give life [John 10:10].

Author of Life

Author and Perfecter of our Faith: [Hebrews 12:2]

Author of Life in the Book of Acts.

Bread of Life: [John 6:35; 6:48]

Bridegroom: [Matthew 9:15]. The picture of Christ as the Bridegroom and the Church as His Bride reveals the special relationship we have with Him. We are bound to each other in a covenant of grace that cannot be broken.

Deliverer: [Romans 11:26]

Good Shepherd: [John 10:11, 14].

High Priest: [Hebrews 2:17]

Lamb of God: [John 1:29] Who takes away the sins of the World.

Rock: [1 Corinthians 10:4]

Resurrection and Life: [John 11:25]

Savior: [Matthew 1:21; Luke 2:11] ***The Way, the Truth, and the Life***: [John 14:6]

Light of the World: [John 8:1]

These Passages come from the Scriptures and they clearly teach us that the Lord Jesus Christ is God, our Creator. Someone may ask or suggest that I, the writer or any other writer present more comments and explain more about the Lord's Deity. Clearly, the Scriptures are the powerful means the Lord gave us to teach us about HIM, to guide us on earth and to teach us about life after death. In my opinion, no one can teach another person about the LORD better than the Word of God, God Himself. Remember that the Lord promises to send the Holy Spirit to teach us about HIM. No one can explain Christ's Deity better than God Himself. *My Lord and My God* considers Scriptures because they are the breathed Word of God and the Holy Spirit Is the best teacher. Consider the Lords' title: ***The Light of the World*** as stated in the Book of John 8:12. Really, if there is no light how can we live? Can this world function? God is Life, He gives us life and He sustains the universe.

We live because the Lord lives and he sustains us [John 14:19; Colossians 1:1.

Conclusion

The Lord IS Alive, the Lord is good to us. No other man has done the works that the Lord Jesus Christ, Our Creator has accomplished including raising the dead and raising Himself from the dead.

Activities for this chapter

1. Which verse (s) convince you that there is Only One God

____

____

____

____

2. Which verse(s) teach you more about Christ's Deity?

____

____

____

____

CHAPTER 9

Bible Verses that Teach that Jesus IS God

> All Scripture is God-breathed and is useful for teaching, rebuking, correcting and training in righteousness, [17] so that the servant of God[a] may be thoroughly equipped for every good work [2 Timothy 3:16-17].

Scriptures are the breathed Word of God [2Timothy 3:16]; they teach us about God's nature, His attributes and His divine plans for humanity. In other words, Scriptures in the Holy Bible teach us about God, our Creator, His creation and His plans for humanity. Scriptures address various subjects regarding deity, divinity; the life hereafter, heaven and hell or inferno. Scriptures are the Word of God and they provide answers to all the questions a human being may have regarding God including the following: Who Is God? What does He do and where does He live? IS there Only One God?

Scriptures answer all these questions clearly and they tell us WHO IS GOD, Our Creator. The fundamental questions that arise in the discussions about God touch on the origin of life: Does God exist? Who Is the God of Creation? Who Is the God of the Bible? In addition, the fundamental questions about God touch on to sin and punishments and on to the life hereafter. Consider the questions below:

1. What happens after death?
2. Is there life after death?
3. Where will I spend eternity?

The best way to answer these questions and to know about our Creator is to read the Word of God, the Holy Scriptures. For examples, when one wants to know if there is Only One God, the Scriptures provide a correct answer to this question as we read: Hear, O Israel: The LORD our God, the LORD is one [Deuteronomy 6:4].

Scriptures teach us that there in Only One God.

When we ask WHO created the world and everything in it, Scriptures teach us that

> The God who made the world and everything in it is the Lord of heaven and earth and does not live in temples built by human hands [Acts 17:24].

And when one wants to know WHO the ONLY GOD OF THE BIBLE IS, Scriptures teach us that the Lord Jesus Christ Is God, our Creator. He is Jehovah Jireh. The Lord says. "I and my Father are ONE" [John 10:30].

Let us consider Powerful passages from the Scriptures that indicate the titles of the LORD from *Torrey's Bible Topics*, and the table *of Juxtaposed Scriptures* compiled by Matt Slick as they teach us that the Lord Jesus Christ IS God, Our Creator.

Please consider, the following titles and names of the Lord Jesus Christ as He is described in the Scriptures, both in the Old Testament and in the New Testament in the following passages. Many scholars have discussed the names and the titles of the Lord Jesus Christ to compile a clear list that can teach that the Lord Jesus Christ is God. Read for yourself about the Lord's names and titles such as Jehovah of Glory, and righteousness, Jehovah above all and many others.

1. Christ is God

    - As Jehovah.

        Isaiah 40:3 The voice of him that crieth in the wilderness, Prepare ye the way of the LORD, make straight in the desert a highway for our God.

Matthew 3:3 For this is he that was spoken of by the prophet Isaiah, saying, The voice of one crying in the wilderness, Prepare ye the way of the Lord, make his paths straight.

- As Jehovah of glory.

Psalms 24:7 Lift up your heads, O ye gates; and be ye lift up, ye everlasting doors; and the King of glory shall come in.

Psalms 24:10 Who is this King of glory? The LORD of hosts, he *is* the King of glory.

- As the Eternal God and Creator.

Psalms 102:24-27 I said, O my God, take me not away in the midst of my days: thy years *are* throughout all generations. 25 Of old hast thou laid the foundation of the earth: and the heavens *are* the work of thy hands. 26 They shall perish, but thou shalt endure: yea, all of them shall wax old like a garment; as a vesture shalt thou change them, and they shall be changed: 27 But thou *art* the same, and thy years shall have no end.

Hebrews 1:8 But unto the Son *he saith*, Thy throne, O God, *is* for ever and ever: a sceptre of righteousness *is* the sceptre of thy kingdom.

Hebrews 1:10-12 And, Thou, Lord, in the beginning hast laid the foundation of the earth; and the heavens are the works of thine hands: 11 They shall perish; but thou remainest; and they all shall wax old as doth a garment; 12 And as a vesture shalt thou fold them up, and they shall be changed: but thou art the same, and thy years shall not fail.

- As the mighty God.

Isaiah 9:6 For unto us a child is born, unto us a son is given: and the government shall be upon his shoulder: and his name shall be called Wonderful, Counseller, The mighty God, The everlasting Father, The Prince of Peace.

- As the Great God and Saviour.

  Hosea 1:7 But I will have mercy upon the house of Judah, and will save them by the LORD their God, and will not save them by bow, nor by sword, nor by battle, by horses, nor by horsemen.

  Titus 2:13 Looking for that blessed hope, and the glorious appearing of the great God and our Saviour Jesus Christ;

- As God over all.

  Psalms 45:6-7 Thy throne, O God, *is* for ever and ever: the sceptre of thy kingdom *is* a right sceptre. 7 Thou lovest righteousness, and hatest wickedness: therefore God, thy God, hath anointed thee with the oil of gladness above thy fellows.

- As the true God.

  Jeremiah 10:10 But the LORD *is* the true God, he *is* the living God, and an everlasting king: at his wrath the earth shall tremble, and the nations shall not be able to abide his indignation.

  1 John 5:20 And we know that the Son of God is come, and hath given us an understanding, that we may know him that is true, and we are in him that is true, *even* in his Son Jesus Christ. This is the true God, and eternal life.

- As God the Word.

  John 1:1 In the beginning was the Word, and the Word was with God, and the Word was God.

- As God, the Judge.

  Ecclesiastes 12:14 For God shall bring every work into judgment, with every secret thing, whether *it be* good, or whether *it be* evil.

> 1 Corinthians 4:5 Therefore judge nothing before the time, until the Lord come, who both will bring to light the hidden things of darkness, and will make manifest the counsels of the hearts: and then shall every man have praise of God.

Several other powerful attributes and titles that are assigned to God, our Creator, and that are also ascribed to our Lord and Savior Jesus Christ include Being Omnipresent, Omnipotent, and Omniscient. God discerns the thoughts in our hearts and the Lord discerns the thoughts in our hearts. All these attributes and titles can be found in both the Old Testament and the New Testament.

Now, just to clarify a few terms, let us remember that being omnipresent means being everywhere at the same time and the Lord Jesus Christ has proven that He can be everywhere at the same time. However, being omnipotent means having all power in heaven and on earth. The Lord Jesus Christ declared that He has authority over the heaven and the earth. As for being omniscient, this attribute means, knowing all, even hidden things and peoples' thoughts. No one else can be omniscient but God, and the Lord Jesus Christ has proven that He knows everything, including the thoughts in human's hearts, in our hearts. The Lord saw the disciple's thoughts. He sees your thoughts and mine.

As for discerning the thoughts in our hearts, this attribute means to know what people think. The Lord Jesus Christ's nature shows all these attributes and titles, therefore, testifying that the Lord Jesus Christ is God, our Creator as we read in the following passages from the King James Bible Version.

Christ is God

- As Omnipresent.

  Matthew 18:20 For where two or three are gathered together in my name, there am I in the midst of them.

  Matthew 28:20 Teaching them to observe all things whatsoever I have commanded you: and, lo, I am with you always, *even* unto the end of the world. Amen.

- As Omnipotent.

  Philippians 3:21 Who shall change our vile body, that it may be fashioned like unto his glorious body, according to the working whereby he is able even to subdue all things unto himself.

  Revelation 1:8 I am Alpha and Omega, the beginning and the ending, saith the Lord, which is, and which was, and which is to come, the Almighty.

- As Omniscient.

  John 16:30 Now are we sure that thou knowest all things, and needest not that any man should ask thee: by this we believe that thou camest forth from God.

  John 21:17 He saith unto him the third time, Simon, *son* of Jonas, lovest thou me? Peter was grieved because he said unto him the third time, Lovest thou me? And he said unto him, Lord, thou knowest all things; thou knowest that I love thee. Jesus saith unto him, Feed my sheep.

- As discerning the thoughts of the heart.

  1 Kings 8:39 Then hear thou in heaven thy dwelling place, and forgive, and do, and give to every man according to his ways, whose heart thou knowest; (for thou, *even* thou only, knowest the hearts of all the children of men;)

  Luke 5:22 But when Jesus perceived their thoughts, he answering said unto them, What reason ye in your hearts?

  Ezekiel 11:5 And the Spirit of the LORD fell upon me, and said unto me, Speak; Thus saith the LORD; Thus have ye said, O house of Israel: for I know the things that come into your mind, *every one of* them.

> John 2:24-25 But Jesus did not commit himself unto them, because he knew all *men*, 25 And needed not that any should testify of man: for he knew what was in man.

If you are not convinced and captivated by the list above that provides you with the titles and the names of our Lord and Savior Jesus Christ, please consider a clear table of compiled Scriptures from the Old Testament and from the New Testament that teach about Christ's Deity and indicate that there is Only One God. This table of compiled Scriptures has been provided by Reverend Matt Slick for religious education.

2. Is Jesus God?

A table of Juxtaposed Scriptures by Matt Slick

"You are my witnesses," declares the LORD, "and my servant whom I have chosen, so that you may know and believe me and understand that I am he. Before me no god was formed, nor will there be one after me." (Isaiah 43:10).

JESUS	**IS**	**GOD, "YAHWEH"**
John 1:3, "Through him all things were made; without him nothing was made that has been made." Col. 1:16-17, "For by him all things were created: things in heaven and on earth, visible and invisible, whether thrones or powers or rulers or authorities; all things were created by him and for him. He is before all things, and in him all things hold together."	Creator	Job 33:4, "The Spirit of God has made me; the breath of the Almighty gives me life." Isaiah 40:28, "Do you not know? Have you not heard? The LORD is the everlasting God, the Creator of the ends of the earth. He will not grow tired or weary, and his understanding no one can fathom."

Rev. 1:17, "When I saw him, I fell at his feet as though dead. Then he placed his right hand on me and said: 'Do not be afraid. I am the First and the Last.'" Rev. 2:8, "To the angel of the church in Smyrna write: These are the words of him who is the First and the Last, who died and came to life again." Rev. 22:13, "I am the Alpha and the Omega, the First and the Last, the Beginning and the End."	First and Last	Isaiah 41:4, "Who has done this and carried it through, calling forth the generations from the beginning? I, the LORD--with the first of them and with the last--I am he." Isaiah 44:6, "This is what the LORD says--Israel's King and Redeemer, the LORD Almighty: I am the first and I am the last; apart from me there is no God." Isaiah 48:12, "Listen to me, O Jacob, Israel, whom I have called: I am he; I am the first and I am the last."
John 8:24, "Therefore I said to you that you will die in your sins; for if you do not believe that I am He, you will die in your sins." (NKJV) John 8:58, "I tell you the truth," Jesus answered, "before Abraham was born, I am!" See Exodus 3:14 John 13:19, "I am telling you now before it happens, so that when it does happen you will believe that I am He."	I AM "ego eimi"	Exodus 3:14, "God said to Moses, "I AM WHO I AM. This is what you are to say to the Israelites: 'I AM has sent me to you.'" Isaiah 43:10, "You are my witnesses," declares the LORD, "and my servant whom I have chosen, so that you may know and believe me and understand that I am he. Before me no god was formed, nor will there be one after me." See also Deut. 32:39

2 Tim. 4:1, "In the presence of God and of Christ Jesus, who will judge the living and the dead, and in view of his appearing and his kingdom, I give you this charge . . ." 2 Cor. 5:10, "For we must all appear before the judgment seat of Christ, that each one may receive what is due him for the things done while in the body, whether good or bad."	Judge	Joel 3:12, "Let the nations be roused; let them advance into the Valley of Jehoshaphat, for there I will sit to judge all the nations on every side." Rom. 14:10, "You, then, why do you judge your brother? Or why do you look down on your brother? For we will all stand before God's judgment seat."
Matt. 2:2, ". . . Where is the one who has been born king of the Jews? We saw his star in the east and have come to worship him." Luke 23:3, "So Pilate asked Jesus, "Are you the king of the Jews?" "Yes, it is as you say," Jesus replied." See also John 19:21	King	Jer. 10:10, "But the LORD is the true God; he is the living God, the eternal King. When he is angry, the earth trembles; the nations cannot endure his wrath." Isaiah 44:6-8, "This is what the LORD says--Israel's King and Redeemer, the LORD Almighty: I am the first and I am the last; apart from me there is no God." See also Psalm 47

John 8:12,"When Jesus spoke again to the people, he said, "I am the light of the world. Whoever follows me will never walk in darkness, but will have the light of life." Luke 2:32, "a light for revelation to the Gentiles and for glory to your people Israel." See also John 1:7-9	Light	Psalm 27:1, "The LORD is my light and my salvation -- whom shall I fear?" Isaiah 60:20,"our sun will never set again, and your moon will wane no more; the LORD will be your everlasting light, and your days of sorrow will end." 1 John 1:5, "God is light; in him there is no darkness at all."
1 Cor. 10:4, ". . . for they drank from the spiritual rock that accompanied them, and that rock was Christ." See also 1 Pet. 2:4-8.	Rock	Deut. 32:4, "He is the Rock, his works are perfect, and all his ways are just. A faithful God who does no wrong, upright and just is he." See also 2 Sam. 22:32 and Isaiah 17:10.
John 4:42, "They said to the woman, 'We no longer believe just because of what you said; now we have heard for ourselves, and we know that this man really is the Savior of the world.'" 1 John 4:14, "And we have seen and testify that the Father has sent his Son to be the Savior of the world."	Savior	Isaiah 43:3, "For I am the LORD, your God, the Holy One of Israel, your Savior" Isaiah 45:21, ". . . And there is no God apart from me, a righteous God and a Savior; there is none but me."

John 10:11, "I am the good shepherd. The good shepherd lays down his life for the sheep."		Psalm 23:1, "The LORD is my shepherd, I shall not be in want."
Heb. 13:20, "May the God of peace, who through the blood of the eternal covenant brought back from the dead our Lord Jesus, that great Shepherd of the sheep . . ." See also John 10:14, 16; 1 Pet. 2:25	Shepherd	Isaiah 40:11, "He tends his flock like a shepherd: He gathers the lambs in his arms and carries them close to his heart; he gently leads those that have young."

This table is clear and it explains itself. After reading the Scriptures above, it is important to examine them, to pray to the Lord, and begin to realize that there is Only One God, and that God does not lie and that Scriptures are the inspired Word of God.

Conclusion

Scriptures don't contradict themselves. The above Scriptures confirm to us that the Lord Jesus Crist is God, our Creator. Believing in Christ's Deity is essential to one's salvation. God is not a man that He should die. God is truth, His Word is Truth [John 17:17].

Activities for this chapter

1. Which passage (s) of the Scripture have convinced you that there is Only One God and that He is our Lord and Savior Jesus Christ? ...

    ____
    ____
    ____
    ____

2. Which passage (s) from the Scriptures, the inspired Word of God are you still doubting?

____
____
____
____

3. In case of doubt, please say a short prayer to the Lord Jesus Christ and present your petition to HIM.

____
____
____
____

4. If you have discovered the truth about the Lord Jesus Christ's Deity, and you believe that there is Only One God Who is the Savior of the world and He is the Lord Jesus Christ, please take time to praise HIM and worship HIM.

____
____
____
____

CHAPTER 10

The Lord's Statements about Himself

Jesus answered: "Don't you know me, Philip, even after I have been among you such a long time? Anyone who has seen me has seen the Father. How can you say, 'Show us the Father'? [John14:9].

Some people believe that the Lord Jesus Christ never claimed to be God, our Creator. They use such arguments that the Lord Jesus called Himself the Son of Man and the Son of God, and that He was constantly praying to His Father.

These arguments are true; however, there is a need to consider other statements that the Lord made regarding His relationship with the Father. Similarly, it is important to consider the meaning of such titles as the Son of Man and the Son of God. It is true that the Lord Jesus Christ called Himself the Son of Man and the Son of God and He was constantly praying to His Father. In fact, in His teachings, the Lord Jesus Christ constantly speaks about God the Father. Let us also remember that the Lord spoke about the Only One God and He stated that "I and the Father are One [John 10:30]"

Before leaving this earth, after He had accomplished His work on earth, while on the cross, the Lord made some powerful statements like, "it is finished [John 19:30] and the very last statement the Lord made when He was on the cross according to Scriptures, the inspired Word of God was: "Father in your Hands I commit my soul" [Luke 23:46]. It is right to consider these verses because they are the inspired Word of God. It is also right to consider all the Scriptures in the discussions about Christ's

Deity including the verses that instruct us about the Lord Jesus Christ's claims about Himself.

Take example of the passage when the Lord said to Philip, "You do not know me since all this time? Whoever has seen me has seen the Father. How can you ask me to show you the Father?" Clearly, the Lord's words in this passage reveal His identity. He cannot be someone else! The Lord was not speaking in parables in the sentence above. When the Lord said, "whoever has seen me has seen the Father," He means it!

I heard of some people saying such thing like, "my best friend is me, he is me and I am him," but at the time of trial, they betray each other. In the case of some fathers who say that they love their sons, that they would do anything for them, there has been always disappointment because at the time of the trials, the father steps back. Let us say that they come to arrest his son, most fathers are likely to let the son get arrested and taken to jail. Then, the father tells his son, I will bring money to bail you out. This is the more logical scenario and response. The Lord and His Father are One. The Lord has never sinned because He is God, Our Creator

The Lord asked: "Who can convince me of sin?"

The fact that the Lord Jesus Christ claims that He forgives sins shows that He is God, our Creator. The Lord Jesus Christ never sinned. He forgives sins.

During His earthly ministry, the Lord Jesus Christ claims that He is God in more than one incident. For example, when the Lord states that in [John 8:24].

> "I said therefore to you, that you shall die in your sins; for unless you believe that I am He, you shall die in your sins."

It is important to see how the Lord deals with the issue of sins

When in the Book of John [8:46-47] the Lord says:

> "Can any of you prove me guilty of sin? If I am telling the truth, why don't you believe me? He who belongs to God hears what God says. The reason you do not hear is that you do not belong to God.

This shows that the Lord is God, our creator.

In addition, the Lord says: "Truly, truly, I say to you, before Abraham was born, I am."

This is exactly what He said to Moses in the Bush when Moses asked God to tell Him His Name

Exodus 3:14, "And God said to Moses, "I AM WHO I A M."

Moreover, we read in Scriptures that God calls the Lord Jesus God.

- Heb. 1:8, "But of the Son He says, "Your throne, O God, is forever and ever, and the righteous scepter is the scepter of His kingdom."

This is evidence from the Scriptures and if anyone questions the statements in the verses above, they question the authority of the Scriptures. No one should question the authority of the Scriptures.

Conclusion

In conclusion, there is Only One God, He is the Lord Jesus Christ as Scriptures teach us.

Activities for this chapter

1. What do you think of the Lord Jesus Christ's claims about Himself?

 ____

 ____

 ____

 ____

2. Why do you think the Lord Jesus Christ accepted to be worshipped?

3. What do you think of the passage in John 10:30 when the Lord Jesus states: "I and the Father are ONE?"

4. Why do you think the Lord Jesus Christ said:?

   "Before Abraham is, I am?" as we read in the Scriptures: "Very truly I tell you," Jesus answered, "before Abraham was born, I am!" [John 8:58]

CHAPTER 11

Who Do You Say Christ Is

> Jesus answered him, "It is also written: 'Do not put the Lord your God to the test.'[d]" [Matthew 4: 7].

The identification of an individual is important to assign statuses and to establish relationships. In the family, in the society and in the world in general, the identification and the statuses matter to establish relationships and orders. Thus, in the family, one finds the father, the mother and the children. An individual can be a father, a husband, a brother, and a friend. All the people who are around an individual and who have some relationships with the individual, must know how to identify this particular individual. The individual can be a son to someone, a husband to another person, and a father to his children. He can also be a sibling and a friend to other people. All the names and relationships teach us about the significance of an identification. An identification determines the statuses, the types of relationships and expectations.

When our Lord and Savior Jesus Christ came to earth, He occupied some positions, as a son of Marie and Joseph. He was also a Brother of John and James: John the Baptist was his cousin and His disciples and His followers called Him Teacher or Master. However, the true identification of our Lord's is found in His name: "Emmanuel, "which means God with us [Matthew 1:23]. The Lords has other names, titles and functions and all of them reveal Who the LORD IS. For example, the name Jesus means the Savior: " She will give birth to a son, and you are to give him the name Jesus,[f] because he will save his people from their sins" [Matthew 1:21].

For his part, the apostle Paul who doubted the teachings of the Lord Jesus Christ for quite a long time, and who even persecuted Christians was surprised when the Lord Jesus Christ appeared to him and asked him the question:

> As he neared Damascus on his journey, suddenly a light from heaven flashed around him. [4] He fell to the ground and heard a voice say to him, "Saul, Saul, why do you persecute me?"
>
> [5] "Who are you, Lord?" Saul asked.
>
> "I am Jesus, whom you are persecuting," he replied. [6] "Now get up and go into the city, and you will be told what you must do" [Acts 9:3-5].

As you can notice in the passage above, Paul had an amazing experience and he recognized the Lord Jesus Christ and he admitted His Sovereignty. Paul become the Lords' Servant and He informs us that every knee shall bow and every tongue will confess that Jesus Christ is Lord:

> Therefore God exalted him to the highest place
> and gave him the name that is above every name,
> [10] that at the name of Jesus every knee should bow,
> in heaven and on earth and under the earth,
> [11] and every tongue acknowledge that Jesus Christ is Lord,
> to the glory of God the Father [Philippians 9:11].

Since Scriptures are the inspired Word of God, they teach the truth and they instruct us that there is Only One God, those who doubt Christ's Deity should read Scriptures and then go to God with a sincere heart and ask God to reveal Himself to them. A simple, plain question that one can ask to the Lord Jesus Christ is: "Lord Jesus, are you my LORD and my GOD?" Or simply say, "Lord Jesus, I doubt that you, I sincerely doubt you are my God and my Lord, will you please reveal yourself to me or send me a passage or passages in Scriptures that will speak to me?"

Since God answers prayers, anyone who approaches Him with a sincere heart, will receive an answer from Him, according to His will because God hears prayers. "Before they call I will answer; while they are still speaking I will hear." [Isaiah 65:24]. God hears prayers and He also answers them: "If you remain in me and my words remain in you, ask whatever you wish, and it will be done for you" [John15:7].

The Word of God is truth and God does not change: "Heaven and earth will pass away, but my words will never pass away" [Matthew 24:35].

It is important to examine Scriptures in order to understand Christ's Deity.

The Lord Jesus told Satan that he created him.

> Jesus answered him, "It is also written: 'Do not put the Lord your God to the test.'[d]" [Matthew 4: 7].

The challenge

It can be difficult to imagine that the Lord God, Our creator Who created the universe humbled Himself, took on flesh and descended to earth to live among the people He created, and even accepted to go to the cross and be crucified to save us. These thoughts are challenging and mind boggling. In addition, imagining that the Lord Jesus Christ is God, our Creator, He Is the Savior of the world and there is salvation in no other name but in the Name of the Lord Jesus Christ can be puzzling. It can be understandable to challenge the thoughts that the Lord Jesus Christ is God, Our Creator, the Creator of the universe and the Only Savior of the World. . Although these thoughts are challenging it does not make it correct because God has provided us with the means to know Him in many ways including through nature and through His divine Word. Although the thought that there is Only One God and He is the Lord Jesus Christ sounds challenging, the doubt is absurd when one fails to study the Word of God to seek for the truth; the doubt is not correct because God asks us to reason with Him. In case of doubt, we need to go to God in prayer and ask Him for guidance.

The best way to know a person or to know about a person is to ask them to tell you who they are. and then you can make your own decision.

During His earthly ministry, Our Lord and Savior Jesus Christ revealed Himself in many circumstances and He told people WHO He IS. For example, during one occasion, the Lord stated that He and the Father are One: "The Father and I and are One." [John 10:30]. On another occasion, the Lord stated that He Who saw Him, has seen the Father. Moreover, on the mount of Transfiguration, the Lord revealed Himself. He also gave Peter the revelation of WHO HE IS and Peter stated that ""You are the Messiah." During the time of temptation, the LORD Stated that HE IS Our Creator. Thomas called Him: My Lord and My God. The Messiah. In other circumstances, the Lord replied that He who sees Him has seen the Father.

Moreover, Scriptures make it clear about the nature of the Lord Jesus Christ. They teach that He is God, our Creator, for example in the following passages we read:

> In the beginning was the Word, and the Word was with God, and the Word was God. [2] He was with God in the beginning. [3] Through him all things were made; without him nothing was made that has been made. [4] In him was life, and that life was the light of all mankind. [5] The light shines in the darkness, and the darkness has not overcome[a] it [John 1-1-5].

The passage that teaches about the supremacy of the Lord Jesus Christ clearly confirms Thomas' statement, "My Lord and My God" as the passage shows that the Lord Jesus Christ is God, our Creator.

> The Son is the image of the invisible God, the firstborn over all creation. [16] *For in him all things were created: things in heaven and on earth, visible and invisible*, whether thrones or powers or rulers or authorities; all things have been created through him and for him. [17] *He is before all things, and in him all things hold together.* [18] And he is the head of the body, the church; he is the beginning and the firstborn from among the dead, so that in everything he might have the supremacy. [19] *For God was pleased to have all his fullness dwell in him,* [20] and through him to reconcile to himself all things, whether things on earth or things in heaven, by making peace through his blood, shed on the cross [Colossians 1:15-20].

The Word of God teaches that there is Only One God Who is the Only Savior of the world. They also teach us that every tongue shall bow and every knee shall confess that Jesus Christ is God.

Thinking that the Lord Jesus Christ is God, our Creator and the Savior of the world can be mind boggling. Even His own disciples did not know WHO HE WAS. We notice this when they were challenged by the most difficult question of the ages when the Lord Jesus Christ asked:

"Who Do You Say I am?

The disciples faced this question and each of them had some kind of answers to this most difficult question: Who do you say Jesus Christ IS?

For his part, the Thomas fell at the Lord's Jesus Christ's Feet and stated: "My Lord and My God."

Scriptures teach us that each one of us will bow and confess that the Lord's Jesus Christ Is God. Before that moment arrives, why don't we face the question today and try to answer it based on the Scriptures. If needs be you can ask the LORD Himself to guide you in your search for answers about His Deity. In the discussion about Christ's Deity, an important point to consider is that Only God Himself reveals His Deity.

If you meet the Lord Jesus Christ today and He asks you one fundamental question: "Who do you Say I am?" The response to this critical question, that refers to life and death, what will your answer be? In other words, what will your answer be to the Lord's question about Who do you say He IS?

And what would you do with the passage that teaches us about Christ's Deity? The one that states that every knee shall bow and every tongue shall confess that Jesus Christ is Lord? [Philippians 9: 2]. A careful examination of the Scriptures confirms that God exists, He is Our Creator, and He is Our Lord and Savior Jesus Christ. God is Eternal and He is immortal.

Conclusion

God exists, He is our Creator. God spoke the world into existence. God created us in His image. The Word of God is Truth [John 17:17].

Activities for this Chapter

1. What answers did the Lord Jesus give to Satan when the later tried to attempt Him?

   ____
   ____
   ____
   ____

2. Which of the answers the Lord gave to Satan impresses you? ……

   ____
   ____
   ____
   ____

3. What do you think of the Lord Jesus Christ's answers to Satan when The Lord says: Do not put the Lord your God to the test.'[d]" [Matthew 4: 7].

   ____
   ____
   ____
   ____

4. What do you think of the Lord address to Satan in the book of Matthew, chapter 4?

   ____
   ____
   ____
   ____

CHAPTER 12

Confessing the Name of the Lord Jesus Christ to Be Saved

> For God so loved the world that he gave his one and only Son, that whoever believes in him shall not perish but have eternal life. [17] For God did not send his Son into the world to condemn the world, but to save the world through him. [18] Whoever believes in him is not condemned, but whoever does not believe stands condemned already because they have not believed in the name of God's one and only Son [John 3:16-18].

We need to confess the name of the Lord Jesus Christ to be saved because Scriptures instruct us that there is salvation in no other name, but in the name of Our Lord and Savior Jesus Christ:

> Salvation is found in no one else, for there is no other name under heaven given to mankind by which we must be saved" [Acts 4:12].

Scriptures are the inspired Word of God and they teach us that there is salvation Only in the Lord Jesus Christ. We are to confess our sins and ask for forgiveness in the name of the Lord Jesus Christ to be saved.

The Blood of the Lord Jesus Christ cleanse us and nullifies our sins. The Blood of the Lord Jesus Christ is the Blood of God:

> Keep watch over yourselves and all the flock of which the Holy Spirit has made you overseers. Be shepherds of the church of God, which he bought with his own blood [Acts 20:28].

Confessing the Name of the Lord Jesus Christ

It is important to repent and to accept the Lord Jesus Christ as one's personal Savior in order to be reconciled with God. If one has not done this yet, there is a need to invite the Lord Jesus Christ in one's heart before one leaves this world. Scriptures teach us that the Lord Jesus Christ is standing at the door and if one invites Him to come to his or her heart, He will come in one's heart [Revel 3:20].

The challenge.

One may ask, what will happen to a person who has not accepted the Lord Jesus Christ as his or her personal Savior? The answer to this question is simple because the Lord Jesus Christ has addressed the issue of salvation and eternal life in His teachings, therefore we can refer to the Lord's teachings to answer the question. During his earthly ministry, the Lord made powerful statements to address various spiritual subjects and questions. These statements help us to answer questions regarding salvation and eternal life.

For example, when the Lord declares that He Is the Way, the Truth, and the Life as we read in Scriptures: [6] Jesus answered, "I am the way and the truth and the life. No one comes to the Father except through me. [7] If you really know me, you will know[b] my Father as well. From now on, you do know him and have seen him." It very clear for us to state that there is only one way to the Father and that salvation is found only in the name of the Lord Jesus Christ [John 14:6].

Elsewhere, the Lord declares that He gives eternal life.

> Whoever eats my flesh and drinks my blood has eternal life, and I will raise them up at the last day [John 6:54].

The Lord also promised to raise His children from the dead.

[40] For my Father's will is that everyone who looks to the Son and believes in him shall have eternal life, and I will raise them up at the last day" [John 6:40].

> Jesus said to her, “I am the resurrection and the life. The one who believes in me will live, even though they die; [John 11:25].
>
> The Lord also promises to give us a glorious bodies [Ephesians2].

The Lord Jesus Christ states that He came to save the world and those who reject Him, the Word of God will be their judge [John 3:16]

Moreover, in John 3:16, Scriptures instruct us about the consequences of rejecting the Lord Jesus Christ. The Lord Jesus Christ said: “There is a judge for the one who rejects me and does not accept my words; the very words I have spoken will condemn them at the last day” [John12:48].

Conclusion

You need to repent and to accept the Lord Jesus Christ as your personal Savior. Repenting and confessing the Name of Our Lord and Savior Jesus Christ are critical for our salvation.

Activities for this Chapter

1. Is there anything that is more important than your soul?

   ____
   ____
   ____
   ____

2. Heaven and hell are real places that are described in the Scriptures. Which of these two places would you like to live in and spend eternity?

   ____
   ____
   ____
   ____

   a. Please make a search to find passages from the Scriptures that describe these two opposite places

b. Where are you going to spend eternity?

3. Who is the Savior of the World according to the Scriptures in the Holy Bible?

____
____
____
____

4. Who do You Say the Lord Jesus Christ IS according to the Scriptures in the Holy?

____
____
____
____

5. How many God, the Creators have you found when you read the Scriptures in the Holy Bible?

____
____
____
____

6. What do you think of the passage of John 1:1-15?

____
____
____
____

7. What words caught your attention when you read the following passages:

   a. [John 1-1-14]?
   b. [Colossians 1:15-20]?

c. [John 10:30]?

____

____

____

____

CHAPTER 13

Lord Jesus Christ, My God and My Creator

> The Son is the image of the invisible God, the firstborn over all creation. [16] For in him all things were created: things in heaven and on earth, visible and invisible, whether thrones or powers or rulers or authorities; all things have been created through him and for him. [17] He is before all things, and in him all things hold together. [18] And he is the head of the body, the church; he is the beginning and the firstborn from among the dead, so that in everything he might have the supremacy. [19] For God was pleased to have all his fullness dwell in him, [20] and through him to reconcile to himself all things, whether things on earth or things in heaven, by making peace through his blood, shed on the cross [Colossians 1:15-19].

Prior to concluding the discussions about the Deity of Our Lord and Savior, Lord Jesus Christ, it is important to recall some important subjects that have been addressed in this book titled, *My Lord and My God*. First, it is important to remind the audience that God exists. He is our Creator and God spoke the world into existence. Secondly, it is important to remember that there is Only One God. Thirdly, it is important to emphasize that the Word of God is powerful and the Word of God is Truth. All the statements above are supported by Scriptures, the inspired Word of God. Lastly, it is also important to point out that the Only God Who is all powerful and Who created the World is our Lord and Savior Jesus Christ as Scriptures teach us. *My Lord and My God* has utilized several passages from the Scriptures to support the point. In other words, the main goal of *My Lord and My God* is to point out that Scriptures teach us that the Lord Jesus Christ is God, Our Creator.

When my publisher gives critics that the book has many citations from the Scriptures, and that there is a need to consider removing some citations, I inform him that the critic is irrelevant because the main goal of this book, *My Lord and My God* is to state that the Lord Jesus Christ is God, Our Creator and our Savior. Therefore, it is important to recall passages from the Scriptures that support the fact that the Lord Jesus Christ is God, our Creator. It was a blessing that my publisher got the message. In some cases, it may be necessary to provide few passages from the Scriptures or try to interpret the Scriptures, but in the case of this book, *My Lord and My God,* it is important to provide more passages from the Scriptures, in both the Old Testament and the New Testament that teach about God's existence, the Only One God to confirm that there is Only One God, and that He is the Lord Jesus Christ. We need to read more passages to understand this powerful truth and to understand why Thomas, one of the Lords' disciples fell at the feet of Our Lord and Savior Jesus Christ and stated, "My LORD and My God." Important to note in this discussions is that Scriptures instruct us that every knee shall bow and every tongue shall confess that the Lord Jesus Christ is LORD as we read in the following passage:

> Therefore God exalted him to the highest place
> and gave him the name that is above every name,
> [10] that at the name of Jesus every knee should bow,
> in heaven and on earth and under the earth,
> [11] and every tongue acknowledge that Jesus Christ is Lord,
> to the glory of God the Father [Philippians 2:9].

Elsewhere, it is written: "'As surely as I live,' says the Lord, 'every knee will bow before me; every tongue will acknowledge God.'" [Romans 14:11].

This is very true because the word of God is Truth. God does not lie.

Considering the truth of the Word of God, the discussions in my this book, *My Lord and My God* lead us to ponder on the critical question Our Lord and Savior Jesus Christ asked His disciples: "Who Do you Say I am?" This is a significant question that everyone needs to ask himself or herself.

Have you ever asked yourself the question: Who do you say Jesus Christ IS? If you have asked yourself this question and you have come upon the right answer supported by the Scriptures, I believe it is a blessing, you should rejoice and continue to worship the Lord in spirt and in truth: "God is spirit, and his worshipers must worship in the Spirit and in truth" [John 4:24].

Now, to continue our discussions about the few subjects that *My Lord and My God.* addresses, we need to start with some powerful truths and facts including the facts that God exists, He is Our Creator, and our Savior. God Loves us and He came to earth to save us. God Is Powerful and His Word is truth.

- ***God exists, He is our Creator***

    That God exists and that He is Our Creator should not be a problem because God's word teaches us that God exists and nature teaches us that God exists and it proclaims His glory [Romans 1:20, Psalms: 19:1]

    For the director of music. A psalm of David. The heavens declare the glory of God; the skies proclaim the work of his hands [Psalml19:1].

We need to believe in God because without faith, it is impossible to please Him. Faith is a gift from God. If one does not believe in God, one can ask God to give him or her faith. The Word of God teaches us to ask [Matthew 7:7].

- ***God is our Creator***

God created the world and everything in it [Acts 4:12]. God spoke the world into existence. God is the Master of the universe; He controls the universe as we read in the Scriptures, the inspired word of God [2 Timothy 3:16].

- **There is Only One God**

Various passages from the Scriptures, in both the Old Testament and the New Testament instruct us that there is Only One God.

- ***The Only God and Savior of the Universe is Our Lord and Savior Jesus Christ***

God, Our Creator, LORD and Savior is Our LORD and SAVIOR JESUS CHRIST. This statement may sound strange, or that the writer is crazy to make such a powerful statement, but the truth of the matter is that Scriptures teach us that the LORD Jesus Christ created us and He Created the universe:

> In the beginning was the Word, and the ***Word was with God,*** and the Word was God. [2] ***He was with God in the beginning.*** [3] Through him all things were made; without him nothing was made that has been made. [4] In him was life, and that life was the light of all mankind. [5] The light shines in the darkness, and the darkness has not overcome[a] it [John 1:1-5].

In the passage above, we are informed that the Word was with God in the beginning, and ***the Word was God.*** This passage delivers the powerful truth, about WHO GOD THE CREATOR IS. What else do we need to read in order to believe that the Lord Jesus Christ is God, Our Creator, and that the LORD created us!

Moreover, the passage of John 1:1-5 instructs us that through the Lord Jesus Christ all things were made, without him nothing was made that has been made.

Elsewhere in the Scriptures in the book of John we read that the Lord Jesus Christ is God, Our Creator [John1:1-5].

The Supremacy of the Son of God

> [15] The Son is the image of the invisible God, the firstborn over all creation. [16] For in him all things were created: things in heaven and on earth, visible and invisible, whether thrones or powers or rulers or authorities; all things have been created through him and for him. [17] He is before all things, and in him all things hold together [Colossians 1:15-17].

Yes, everything was created by Him and for Him and, the fullness of God dwells in Him. These facts teach the powerful truth of Christ's Deity.

- Christ's Deity and the Attributes of God

Also important to consider in the discussions about Christ's Deity are the attributes of God. God has many attributes which are facts

- God IS Eternal.
- God IS Truth.
- God IS Holy.
- God IS Omniscient.
- God IS Omnipotent.
- God is Omnipresent.

These attributes and God's other attributes teach us about God's nature and God's identity. When one reads the scriptures to compare verses about such things as the attributes of God found in the Old Testament that include His Eternity, Omnipotence, Omniscience, as well as Righteousness, and compare these attribute to the attributes of the Lord Jesus Christ in the New Testament, one will notice that all the attributes of God apply to the LORD JESUS CHRIST completely.

These are facts related in Scriptures. WHO Is Eternal, but GOD!

In the Old Testament, the Lord God is called Eternal God, and in the New Testament, the LORD Jesus Christ is called the Eternal God.

In the Old Testament, the LORD GOD is the omniscient, the Holy ONE who knows the end of things before they begin. In the New Testament, the LORD Jesus Christ is the Omniscient God who knows everything. He knew people's thoughts. He never sinned and He is the Anointed ONE. He is the Savior of the world. He forgives sins and He raises people from death! He was worshipped, He accepted worship and He is prayed to. The Lord performed miracles that no one else could do, but GOD, HIMSELF, testifying that He is God our Creator!

- ***God Is Truth***

God is Truth and His Word Is Truth. The Lord Jesus Christ said that He Is the Way, the Truth and the Life. If God is Truth and the Lord Jesus is Truth, we can conclude that the Lord Jesus Christ is God, Our Creator.

In conclusion, we can say that the best tool to consider in the discussions about Christ's Deity is the Scriptures because they are the inspired Word of God and they proclaim the truth and they are truth [2 Peter, John 17:17]. The Word of God is truth because what God says comes to pass and the Word of God never returns to Him void. Furthermore, God has provided evidence that testifies to the truth of His Word.

To further discuss about the truth of the Word of God, let us consider the discussions in the following paragraphs:

I. Scriptures teach that The Word of God is Truth

Prior to discussing the truth of the Word of God, let us agree that God exists. The Word of God teaches us that God exists and that He loves us. God loves us so much that He created us in His own image [Genesis 2:27] and God loves us to the point that when our first parents, Adam and Eve disobeyed Him, God took on Flesh to become Man like us and He came to earth to save us, this is the message we read in the passage of [John 1:1-5]. In addition, in the same Book of John and in the same chapter, [John 1:1-14[, Scriptures instruct us that when God came to this world, the world did not recognize Him. These are powerful messages from the Scriptures.

Moreover, throughout the scriptures in the Holy Bible, we find powerful passages that give a clear indication that God exists, He is our Creator and He loves us. There is Only One God, the Lord Jesus Christ is God, our Creator. Now, whether one believes this powerful truth from the Scriptures or not, it does not change the truth. The truth will always remain the truth. It was the Lord Jesus Christ who stated that the Word of God is truth [John 17:17].

The Lord also stated that He is the Truth, the Way and the Life and that no one goes to the Father, except through Him:

> Jesus answered, "I am the way and the truth and the life. No one comes to the Father except through me [John 14:6].

This powerful passage from the Scriptures has been repeatedly mentioned to emphasize the truth the Lord Jesus Christ is God, Our Creator.

The Lord Jesus Christ preached with authority, this can clearly indicate to us that He is God, our Creator. When Thomas, one of the Lord's disciples fell at His Feet and called HIM, My Lord and my God, he received the revelation and he was simply confirming the truth.

Scriptures instruct us that the Lord Jesus Christ is God and that He is our Creator. The goal of this book, *My Lord and My God,* is to confirm that God exists and He is Our creator; the Word God is Truth; God created the world and everything in it [Acts 17: 24]; and God who created the universe, the world and everything in it, is the Lord Jesus Christ as Scriptures teach us.

The Lord Jesus Christ is God, Our Creator, He is Our Lord and Our Savior.

All Scriptures that teach us about Christ's Deity, deliver powerful messages about the Lord's identity and they instruct us that the Lord Jesus Christ is our God, our Creator, and our Savior. As examples, we can consider the messages that revealed our LORD's identity in the following passages of the Scriptures in various circumstances:

- When the Lord Jesus Christ stated that before Abraham was, HE IS. "I AM."

This is a powerful statement. How could it be possible when the Lord was not even 50 years old? Abraham looked older than Him. How could this possibly be, unless He is the ONE WHO created Abraham and sent Abraham to fulfill His missions on earth!

- During the time of His temptation The Lord Jesus Christ told Satan that, "it is written, do not tempt the Lord, your God."

Now, when the Lord Jesus told Satan, it is also written, don't tempt God, your Creator, clearly the Lord indicated that He is God, Our Creator and He created Satan.

You can imagine what happened when the Lord quoted this powerful passage from the Scriptures, Satan ran away. Any creature could run away too. How can you argue with your Creator when He knows you more than you even know yourself!

Scriptures reveal a lot about the nature of our LORD. Wait until you read a few more statements that the LORD made. Consider the following question when the Lord asked the crowd.

- Who can convict me of sin? The Lord asked.

  This means that the Lord never sinned, therefore, He is God. Clearly, only God has never sinned.

When you reflect on the question the Lord asked in this passage, it is mind blowing. Have you ever met or heard about anyone who has never sinned except God?

Well, Scriptures teach us that the Lord Jesus Christ has never sinned, therefore, the Lord Jesus Christ is God.

The Lord Jesus Christ has never sinned, but He forgives sins. Similarly, the Lord Jesus Christ is the Author of Life and He gives life as we read in the Book of Acts [20:28] and in the Book of John [10:10]. The Lord forgives sins:

> "This is my blood of the covenant, which is poured out for many for the forgiveness of sins. [Matthew 26:28]. The Lord shared His Precious Blood to forgive our sins
>
> Keep watch over yourselves and all the flock of which the Holy Spirit has made you overseers. Be shepherds of the church of God, which he bought with his own Blood [Acts 20:28].

II. The Lord Jesus Christ has the power to forgive sins

Forgiveness of sins.

The Lord declared that He has the power to forgive sins. Only God forgives sins. Now, because the Lord forgives sins, the Lord is God. There are numerous passages that blow our minds. For examples:

- The Lord Jesus Christ was worshipped Matthew [2;2:2,11;14:33: 28] Only God can be worshipped, because the Lord Jesus accepted to be worshipped, this clearly shows that the Lord Jesus Christ is God, Our Creator.
- The Lord Jesus Christ was prayed to, Acts 7:59; 1 Cor. 1:1:2. We can only pray to God. But in Scriptures, we read that the Lord was prayed to. For example, when Stephen was stoned to death, he prayed to the Lord Jesus Christ as we read in the Book of Acts.
- The Lord Jesus Christ was called God [John 1:2; John 20; 28; Hebrews 1:8].
- The Lord Jesus Christ was called the Son of God, [Mark 1:1]. The Son of God means God.
- The Lord Jesus Christ never sinned. He was sinless [1 Peter 2; 22; Hebrews 4:15]
- The Lord Jesus Chris is Omniscient, He knows all things as we read in the book of [John 21:17]. Only God knows everything. He knows our thoughts and He sees our thoughts. This is scary! If someone is still refuses to accept that the Lord Jesus Christ is God, Our Creator. That person is rejecting Scriptures because Scriptures instruct us about the Lord Jesus Christ. During His earthly ministry when some people were doubting Him, the Lord took the Scroll and He told them that the Scriptures were written about Him.
- The Lord Jesus Christ gives eternal life. He gives eternal life [John 10:28]. Scriptures teach us that the Lord Jesus Christ gives eternal life. Evidently, we need the LORD to obtain eternal life,
- The fullness of Deity dwells in the Lord Jesus Christ. [Colossians 2:9]. This is one of the powerful Scriptures that makes things clear. The fullness of the Deity, the fullness of God dwells in the

Lord Jesus Christ! This passage makes it clear that, the Lord is our God, our creator.

- Every knee shall bow and every tongue shall confess that the Lord Jesus Christ is God. This message is also very clear, every knee shall bow and every tongue shall confess that the Lord Jesus Christ is God.

As one reads the Scriptures, one realizes that the Word of God is powerful and the Word of God is truth [John 17:17]. It was the Lord Jesus Christ who stated that the Word of God is Truth. The Lord stated this powerful statement in the High Priest Prayer,

The Lord Jesus Christ had the nature of God and the nature of man.

He was conceived by the Holy Spirit when He took on Flesh. His Father and Him Are One.

Even the verses that indicate that the Lord Jesus Christ was called Man deliver powerful information that cause one to ponder. For examples when the Lord worshiped the Father, He stated powerful statements such as "the glory I had with you before the world began: "[5] And now, Father, glorify me in your presence with the glory I had with you before the world began." [John 17:5]. Wow! This is a powerful statement! Who could make such statement if not God Himself?

Through Him everything was made, nothing that has been made was made without Him. This is a citation from the book of John.

This passage from the Scriptures [John1:1-5], clearly teaches us that the Lord Jesus Christ is God, Our Creator who created the heaven and the earth and everything in it. No matter how in doubt one may be, the above passage presents a solid argument to teach us about Christ's Deity, and that cannot be doubted. One does not need to be highly educated to understand that everything was made by the Lord Jesus Christ and that everything was made through Him and nothing that was made was made without Him. This passage is mind blowing. When I read this passage during my devotions, usually in the morning, I wonder and I ponder, how this passage did not get my attention for many years when it is so clear!

Similarly, I wonder, if most people who have been resisting to accept that the Lord Jesus Christ is God, Our Creator have read this passage of John 1-5? More precisely, the words in the passage that reads ' In the beginning was the Word, and the Word was with God, and the Word was God. [2] He was with God in the beginning. [3] Through him all things were made; without him nothing was made that has been made. [4] In him was life, and that life was the light of all mankind. [5] The light shines in the darkness, and the darkness has not overcome[a] it.

As we can see all things were created by Him and for Him. Nothing that has been made has been made without HIM! Oh! My God.

How clearly do we want God to teach us that He is the Lord Jesus Christ? One may wonder!

Do we wish for God to come down from heaven to teach us in a classroom or to minister to us in the market places when He has given us His Word to teach us and His Holy Spirit to instruct us? In addition, God has provided leaders to teach us the Word of God in truth.

Conclusion

The Lord Jesus Christ Is God, Our Creator and He loves us as the Scriptures instruct us. Only God Himself has the ability to save us and to redeem us from our sins. The redemption from sins required the Blood of God because only God has never sinned.

Activities for this chapter

1. Make a list of things that the Lord has done for you in your life that show His love for you.

   ____
   ____
   ____
   ____

2. Make a list of verse (s) from the Scriptures that minister to you more about God's love for you and for the world.

____
____
____
____

CHAPTER 14

The Significance of the Passage of John 1-5 in the New Testament

> In the beginning was the Word, and the Word was with God, and the Word was God. [2] He was with God in the beginning. [3] Through him all things were made; without him nothing was made that has been made. [4] In him was life, and that life was the light of all mankind. [5] The light shines in the darkness, and the darkness has not overcome[a] it [John 1:1-5].

It is interesting to know that there are many scholars who have pointed to the passage of [John 1:1-5] as the powerful passage of the Bible that speaks about creation and tells us who the Creator IS. I am here remembering the writing of Philip Johnson in his book titled Defeating Darwinism as he addresses the issue of the origin of life and states that God exists, He created the universe and that God who created the universe is our Lord and Savior Jesus Christ [Johnson 1997] It is true that the subjects of God's existence and creation are discussed throughout the Scriptures in the Holy Bible. For example, the Book of Genesis starts with powerful words:

In the Beginning as we read in the passage below.

> In the beginning God created the heavens and the earth. [2] Now the earth was formless and empty, darkness was over the surface of the deep, and the Spirit of God was hovering over the waters.
>
> [3] And God said, "Let there be light," and there was light. [4] God saw that the light was good, and he separated the light from the

> darkness. [5] God called the light "day," and the darkness he called "night." And there was evening, and there was morning—the first day. … [Genesis 1:1-6].

In comparison, the Book of John starts with powerful words: "In the Beginning":

In the beginning was the Word, and the Word was with God, and the Word was God [John 1:1-1]

This passage is also similar to the passage in the Book of Genesis

> In the beginning God created the heavens and the earth [Genesis 1:1]

There is Only One God. The Lord Jesus Christ.

Conclusion

Most scholars believe that the passage of John 1: 1-5 clearly teaches us that the Lord Jesus Christ Is God, He Is God, our Creator.

Activities for this chapter

1. What do you think of the passage of John 1:1-5?

   ____
   ____
   ____
   ____

2. Make a list of verses that teach that there is only One God.

   ____
   ____
   ____
   ____

CHAPTER 15

The Attributes of God

> "You know what is in everyone's heart. So from your home in heaven answer their prayers, according to the way they live and what is in their hearts." [I Kings 8:39].

God knows everything and God sees everything.

The eyes of the LORD are in every place, watching the evil and the good [Proverbs 15:3].

One of the important factors to consider in the discussions of Christ's Deity is the attributes of God because the attributes of God are unique characteristics that are applied only to God, our Creator and all these unique attributes of God are described in the Scriptures, the inspired Word of God, they include immutability as God does not change. This characteristic is also attributed to the Lord Jesus Christ as it is written that the Lord Jesus Christ is the same yesterday, today tomorrow and forever [Hebrews 13:8].

God	**Jesus**
God Never Changes	Jesus never Changes
Malachi 3:6 For I am the LORD, I change not; therefore ye sons of Jacob are not consumed.	Hebrews 13:8 Jesus Christ the same yesterday, and today, and forever.

When I was a young believer, I was often interested in the characteristics of the Lord Jesus Christ because He never changes. I was very impressed by the fact that the miracles the Lord accomplished in the past, He can accomplish them even today. For examples healing the sick, answering prayers and feeding the crowd. As most Christians can testify, the Lord Jesus Christ does not change. I used to love the powerful verse of Hebrews 13. In French, we recognize the immutable nature of our Lord and Savior Jesus Christ by referring to the Lord as *[Heubreux 13:8].* A powerful and amazing verse that refers to the Lord Jesus Christ's Character!

Now, as I became mature in Christ, I learned that God does not change which leads me to the conclusion that the Lord Jesus Christ is God, our Creator.

While considering the attributes of the Lord, I should admit that as a young believer, I thought that the Lord Jesus Christ was forgiving and the Father, a God of wrath. In other words, I was afraid of God the Father. I was thinking that God punishes sins and that the Lord Jesus Christ forgives sins. I remember very well having a conversation with a friend who was a young believer, as well and who laughed at me because of my ignorance. But by God's grace, as I grew spiritually, the Lord has been helping me to know that there is only one God. I praise the Lord for assisting me because this confusion could obstruct my faith.

First of all, let us ask the question, "What is the Nature of God?" According to Scriptures God is Spirt, God is the Word. This is also the nature of the Lord Jesus Christ as we can see in the following lines in the table below:

God	**Jesus**
God is the Word. In the beginning was the Word, and the Word was with God, and the Word was God [John 1:1].	Jesus is the Word ...the Word was made flesh, and dwelt among us...[John 1:14].

Another characteristic worth mentioning about the Lord is that He Is Almighty, God the Creator. Now, when you ask someone who created the world, they will tell you God, but what are some of the other names of God? They will not tell you that He is the Lord Jesus Christ, Immanuel, God with us. Not all people accept this powerful truth, but let us examine the Scriptures to see what they say about God, Our Creator as we seek to answer the question about who created the universe. According to Scriptures, God alone created the universe and the universe exists by His power.

Now, let us look at the Scriptures in the table below to see what they teach us about WHO IS the Creator. The following passages come from the King James Version of the Bible.

God	**Jesus**
God created the universe and earth by Himself.	Jesus Christ created the universe and the earth.
I am the LORD that maketh all things; that stretcheth forth the heavens alone; that spreadeth abroad the earth by myself. [Isaiah 44:24].	[U]nto the Son he saith...Thou, LORD, in the beginning hast laid the foundation of the earth; and the heavens are the works of thine hands. [Hebrews 1:10]
In the beginning God created the heaven and the earth [Genesis 1:1]	[B]y him [Jesus] were all things created, that are in heaven, and that are in earth...all things were created by him, and for him. [Colossians 1:16]
	All things were made by him; and without him was not anything made that was made [John 1:3].

Holiness

That God is Holy should not be a problem for anyone because He is Holy and He has never sinned as scriptures instruct us. Scriptures teach us that God is Holy, and they teach that the Lord Jesus Christ is Holy, as we can read in the passages below:

God	Jesus
God Is the Holy ONE	**Jesus is the Holy One**
Psalms 71:22 I will also praise thee with the psaltery, even thy truth,O my God: unto thee will I sing with the harp, O thou Holy One of Israel. Psalms 78:41 Yea, they turned back and tempted God, and limited the Holy One of Israel. Psalms 89:18 For the LORD is our defence; and the Holy One of Israel is our king. Isaiah 10:20 And it shall come to pass in that day, that the remnant of Israel, and such as are escaped of the house of Jacob, shall no more again stay upon him that smote them; but shall stay upon the LORD, the Holy One of Israel, in truth. Psalms 16:10 For thou wilt not leave my soul in hell; neither wilt thou suffer thine Holy One to see corruption. (Messianic Psalm).	Acts 2:27 Because thou wilt not leave my soul in hell, neither wilt thou suffer thine Holy One to see corruption. 3:13-14 The God of Abraham, and of Isaac, and of Jacob, the God of our fathers, hath glorified his Son Jesus; whom ye delivered up, and denied him in the presence of Pilate, when he was determined to let him go. But ye denied the Holy One and the Just, and desired a murderer to be granted unto you; 13:34-35 And as concerning that he raised him up from the dead, now no more to return to corruption, he said on this wise, I will give you the sure mercies of David. Wherefore he saith also in another psalm, Thou shalt not suffer thine Holy One to see corruption.

Also important to remember here is the worship issue. Scriptures teach clearly that we are to only worship God, not anyone else. And God Himself instructs us to worship HIM alone.

Equally important is the power to forgive sins and the power to raise people from dead.

Let us first consider the forgiveness of sins. Who can forgive sins but God Himself!

Scriptures teach us that God forgives sins and that the Lord Jesus Christ forgives sins as well as we read in the passages from the Scriptures in the table below:

God	**Jesus**
God forgives sins.	Jesus Forgives sins.
Praise the LORD, my soul; all my inmost being, praise his holy name. 2 Praise the LORD, my soul, and forget not all his benefits— 3 who forgives all your sins and heals all your diseases, 4 who redeems your life from the pit and crowns you with love and compassion, 5 who satisfies your desires with good things so that your youth is renewed like the eagle's. The Lord..forgiveth all thine iniquities... [Psalm 103:2-3] "Who can forgive sins but God only?" [Mark 2:7].	Jesus forgives sins. When Jesus saw their faith, he said to the paralyzed man, "*Son, your sins are forgiven*"[Mark 2:5]. When Jesus saw their faith, he said, "Friend, your sins are forgiven"[Luke 5:20]. Then Jesus said to her, "Your sins are forgiven" [Luke 7:48]. Some men brought to him a paralyzed man, lying on a mat. When Jesus saw their faith, he said to the man, "Take heart, son; your sins are forgiven" [Matthew 9:2].

God	**Jesus**
God is the Messiah ...unto us a child is born, unto us a son is given: and the government shall be upon his shoulder...and his name shall be called... The mighty God, The everlasting Father... [Isaiah 9:6]	Jesus is the Messiah The woman saith unto him, I know that Messiah cometh, which is called Christ: when he is come, he will tell us all things. Jesus saith unto her, I that speak unto thee am he [John 4:25-26]

God	Jesus
Only God is glorified. I am the LORD: that is my name: and my glory will I not give to another...[Isaiah 42:8]	God glorified Jesus. And now, O Father, glorify thou me with thine own self with the glory which I had with thee before the world was. John 17:5 [All men should honour the Son, even as they honour the Father. He that honoureth not the Son honoureth not the Father which hath sent him [John 5:23] But unto the Son he [God] saith, Thy throne, O God, is for ever and ever: a sceptre of righteousness is the sceptre of thy kingdom. [Hebrews 1:8]

God is said to be Everlasting and the Lord Jesus Christ is said to be Everlasting as we read in the Scriptures.

God	Jesus
God is from everlasting. The LORD reigneth, he is clothed with majesty; the LORD is clothed with strength, wherewith he hath girded himself: the world also is stablished, that it cannot be moved. Thy throne is established of old: thou art from everlasting [Psalms 93:1-2]	Jesus is from everlasting. But thou, Bethlehem Ephratah... out of thee shall he come forth unto me that is to be ruler in Israel; whose goings forth have been from of old, from everlasting [Micah 5:2]

How can one be everlasting and not be God? The passages above clearly show that God is Eternal and that there is Only One God

There is Only One Savior. Scriptures teach that God is the Only Savior and they also teach that the Lord Jesus Christ is the Only Savior:

God	**Jesus**
God is the only Saviour. "I, even I, am the LORD; and beside me there is no saviour." Isaiah 43:11 To the only wise God our Saviour... Jude 1:12 God our Saviour. Titus 2:10 ...we trust in the living God, who is the Saviour. I Timothy 4:10 God my Saviour. Luke 1:47	Jesus is the only Saviour. ...the Father sent the Son to be the Saviour of the world. 1 John 4:14 ...our Lord and Saviour Jesus Christ. II Peter 3:18 ...God and our Saviour Jesus Christ. II Peter 1:1 ...the Christ, the Saviour of the world. John 4:42 ...the Lord Jesus Christ our Saviour. Titus 1:4 a Saviour, which is Christ the Lord. Luke 2:11 Neither is there salvation in any other (than Jesus): for there is none other name under heaven given among men, whereby we must be saved. --Acts 4:12 ...salvation... is in Christ Jesus with eternal glory. --2 Timothy 2:10 ...captain of their salvation [Jesus] perfect through sufferings. [-- Heb 2:10]. [Jesus]...author of eternal salvation... [-- Heb 5:9]

Similarly, we read in the Scriptures that God is the Redeemer and the Lord Jesus Christ is the Redeemer.

God	Jesus
God is our Redeemer. [T]hou, O LORD, art our father, our redeemer. [Isaiah 63:16]	Jesus Redeemed us. [T]the great God and our Saviour Jesus Christ...gave himself for us, that he might redeem us from all iniquity [Titus 2:13-14]

God is One There is Only One God

God	Jesus
God is one. Hear, O Israel: The LORD our God is one LORD. [Deuteronomy 6:4]	Jesus and God are one. I and my Father are one. John 10:30 In the beginning was the Word, and the Word was with God, and the Word was God...All things were made by him...He was in the world, and the world was made by him, and the world knew him not...And the Word was made flesh, and dwelt among us [John 1:1, 3, 10, 14]. Jesus saith...he that hath seen me hath seen the Father; and how sayest thou then, Shew us the Father? [John 14:9] For there are three that bear record in heaven, the Father, the Word, and the Holy Ghost: and these three are one. [1 John 5:7].

God	Jesus
God is the first and the last. I the LORD, the first, and with the last; I am he. Isaiah 41:4	Jesus is the first and the last. Jesus said, "Fear not; I am the first and the last:" Revelation 1:17

God	Jesus
God heals all diseases. Bless the LORD...who healeth all thy diseases. Psalms 103:2	Jesus heals all diseases. [Jesus] healed all that were sick. Matthew 8:16

Life, God has life in Himself Jesus has life in Himself

God	Jesus
God has life in Himself. [T]he Father hath life in himself; John 5:26	Jesus has life in Himself. so hath [God] given to the Son to have life in himself; In [Jesus] was life; and the life was the light of men. John 1:4

Scriptures also teach us that God raises the dead and Jesus raised the dead

God	Jesus
God raises the dead. [T]he Father raiseth up the dead, and quickeneth them; John 5:21	Jesus raises the dead. [T]he Son quickeneth whom he will. John 5:21

It is written that God is "I AM" and the Lord Jesus Christ is also "AM"

God	Jesus
God is the Great "I AM" And God said unto Moses, I AM THAT I AM: and he said, Thus shalt thou say unto the children of Israel, I AM hath sent me unto you. [Exodus 3:14]	Jesus is the Great "I AM" Jesus said unto them, Verily, verily, I say unto you, Before Abraham was, I am. [John 8:58].

The Lord Jesus Christ is also called Son of God and Son of Man. As we read in the Scriptures [John 5:18].

Now, it is clear that God has A Son. The Son of God is Messiah. During His earthly ministry, when the Lord Jesus Christ stated that He is the Son of God, the Pharisees wanted to stone Him because the Son of God is Messiah and Messiah is God Himself. Truly Scriptures cannot contradict themselves because the Word of God is truth.

God	Jesus
God has a Son. [T]he LORD hath said unto me, Thou art my Son; this day have I begotten thee. Psalms 2:7	Jesus is God's Son. ... [Jesus] said also that God was his Father... John 5:18

Son of God means Messiah, God Himself.

It is important to examine another fundamental statement which is related to God's Sovereignty and authority regarding Judgement and the Lord Jesus Christ deity. Scriptures teach us that God is the Judge. God will Judge the world. Similarly, they teach us that the Lord Jesus Christ is the

Judge

God	Jesus
God is the Judge of the whole earth. O Lord God, to whom vengeance belongeth; O God, to whom vengeance belongeth, shew thyself. Lift up thyself, thou judge of the earth: render a reward to the proud. Psalms 94:1-2 [Abraham to God]...Shall not the Judge of all the earth do right? Genesis 18:25	Jesus is the Judge of the whole earth. [T]he Father judgeth no man, but hath committed all judgment unto the Son: John 5:22

The Lord Himself said that the Word will judge. We know that the Word is God.

This absolute truth cannot be denied.

The Lord Jesus Christ is God, Our Creator. Everything that was created by Him and for Him as we read in the Book of Colossians 1:15.

The Lord Jesus Created Satan.

To conclude the Lord Jesus Christ is God our Creator, Because He created the universe and the world is held by Him.

> The Son is the image of the invisible God, the firstborn over all creation. [16] For in him all things were created: things in heaven and on earth, visible and invisible, whether thrones or powers or rulers or authorities; all things have been created through him and for him. [17] He is before all things, and in him all things hold together. [18] And he is the head of the body, the church; he is the beginning

> and the firstborn from among the dead, so that in everything he might have the supremacy. [19] For God was pleased to have all his fullness dwell in him [Colossians 1:15-20].

Conclusion

Scriptures teach that there is only One God. A closer examination of the Scriptures also reveals that the Lord Jesus Christ is God our Creator. His nature and his attributes confirm this powerful truth.

Activities

1. Which passage (s) from the Scriptures convince you that God exists?

 ____
 ____
 ____
 ____

2. Which passage (s) convince you that there is Only One God?

 ____
 ____
 ____
 ____

 Write down the attributes of God, underline, these attributes of God that you like and compare them to the attributes of the Lord Jesus Christ and state how many God the attributes refer to.

 ____
 ____
 ____
 ____
 ____

CHAPTER 16

The Lord Jesus Christ's Attributes

> Knowing their thoughts, Jesus said, "Why do you entertain evil thoughts in your hearts? [Matthew 9:4]

The Lord Jesus Christ is Omniscient; He knows the thoughts in our hearts.

In the discussions about Christ's Deity or the divinity of the Lord Jesus Christ, one thing remains clear and mind blowing, that is that, the Lord Jesus Christ has the attributes of God. These attributes cannot be applied to anyone else, but to God our creator, the creator of the universe. Consider for examples, the omniscient nature and attribute of God. Everyone who believes in God knows that God knows everything; and He even knows the motives and the intensions of our hearts. Scriptures instruct us that nothing in all creation is hidden from God's sight as we read in the Book of Hebrews [4:12]. Also, in the Book of Psalm (139), we read that God perceives our thoughts from afar. Simply put, God knows everything including the thoughts in our hearts. God knows everything and He sees everything as we read in the Scriptures:

> [1] You have searched me, LORD,
> and you know me.
> [2] You know when I sit and when I rise;
> you perceive my thoughts from afar.
> [3] You discern my going out and my lying down;
> you are familiar with all my ways.
> [4] Before a word is on my tongue
> you, LORD, know it completely.
> [5] You hem me in behind and before,

> and you lay your hand upon me.
> [6] Such knowledge is too wonderful for me,
> too lofty for me to attain.
> [7] Where can I go from your Spirit? [Psalm 139:1-6].

Keeping these words in mind, we also read that the Word of God is God and the Word of God is Alive.

> For the word of God is alive and active. Sharper than any double-edged sword, it penetrates even to dividing soul and spirit, joints and marrow; it judges the thoughts and attitudes of the heart. [13] Nothing in all creation is hidden from God's sight. Everything is uncovered and laid bare before the eyes of him to whom we must give account [Hebrews 4:12].

This is scary and powerful because the Word of God is truth. Now, let us remember that the Word of God is our Lord and Savior Jesus Christ as we read in the Book of [John 1:1-2].

We believe that God knows everything and that He sees everything. This is true because the Word of God is truth [John17:17] and God has provided us with evidence that testifies to His omniscience attribute as well as to His other attributes.

Regarding Scriptures teaching about the truth of the Word of God, the Lord Jesus instructs us in the Book of John that the Word of God is truth. This is a matter of faith in God. One needs to believe this powerful truth based on his or her faith in God, the love for God and the willingness to obey God. In case of doubts and challenges, ONYLY GOD can address this problem. Faith in God is a gift from God as Scriptures teach us. As a matter of fact, the Lord Jesus said that apart from Him, we cannot do anything:

> I am the vine; you are the branches. If you remain in me and me in you, you will bear much fruit; apart from me you can do nothing [John 15:5].

When I think about this passage, in my humble opinion, I believe that even to believe in God, we need the Lord's assistance. Please don't quote me on this one. In my humble opinion, I am convinced that we are saved by grace. God calls us to Him by grace and everything we obtain is by grace. If the Lord said that apart from Him, we cannot do anything, this indeed means anything, including faith in Him. I may be exaggerating here, but the truth of the matter is that faith is a gift from God. We are saved by grace. Another passage in the Scripture worth mentioning is, no one comes to me, unless the father calls Him:

> Jesus answered, "I am the way and the truth and the life. No one comes to the Father except through me. [John14:6].

To believe in God and be willing to obey His commands is a matter of grace and a gift from God. Therefore, one needs God's assistance to believe that His Word is Truth.

God has provided evidence that has testified to the power and the truth of His Word. Just think about what God told Adam in the Garden of Eden concerning the forbidden tree that he must not eat from. God said to Adam that the day he would eat from the forbidden tree, he would die. Just as God said, when Adam and Eve ate from the forbidden tree, they died. Have you ever wondered why death is around us, we lose our loved ones, people die, and we are doomed to die and return to dust? It all started in the Garden of Eden when Adam and Eve disobeyed God and brought curse into the world. Certainly, this confirms the truth and the power of the Word of God. God is truth and He speaks truth. Whatever God says happens just as He says.

Most scholars believe that Adam and Even first died spiritually, immediately, as God spoke to them and then, they died physically and the earth was cursed. Now, why is there suffering in the world and we experience death, one may ask. The answer is found in the Scriptures, the inspired Word of God as we read in the Book of Genesis:

> ...but you must not eat from the tree of the knowledge of good and evil, for when you eat from it you will certainly die" [Genesis 2:17].

The Word of God is truth, because Scriptures are truth and they teach that God knows the end of things before they even begin:

> I make known the end from the beginning, from ancient times, what is still to come. I say, 'My purpose will stand, and I will do all that I please [Isaiah 46:10].

God knew that Adam and Eve would disobey Him and He would come to earth to redeem us; God knew this because He is an Omniscient God.

Concerning the evidence that God has provided to testify to the Truth of His Word, many peoples agree that there are many things that God has done to reveal Himself to people and to testify to the power and to the truth of His Word: God reveals Himself through nature, in dreams and in visions. God has also revealed Himself through the Lord Jesus Christ when He took on Flesh to become Human and to live among us, and was called Immanuel, God with us.

God has revealed to many what they did not know or were aware. God by His grace has revealed the hidden secrets to them in miraculous ways. The events or messages God may reveal to His children by grace are numerous, ranging from deep secrets and hidden event, secrets of the hearts, the thoughts in our hearts and anything you can imagine. God can even reveal to a married person whose wife or husband is cheating that the partner is not being faithful. Even when a couple is not yet in a serious relationship, but simply thinking of engaging in a serious relationship, God can choose to reveal to one partner the secrets that the other partner is hiding. I remember one day, when a brother in Christ, I will call Bill, shared with me how the Lord had helped him to find out that his wife was engaged in an inappropriate relationship with a doctor who was giving him treatments when he was hospitalized. Brother Bill said that he was disappointed, he was scared, and he confronted his wife, but she denied about the affairs. He remained in the hospital for a few days, but later, he requested to be discharged from the hospital.

He believed that the Lord revealed his wife's affair with the doctor in a dream, which he was not aware of, and was surprised. How could a woman he loved so much, the mother of his children could love another man while she is still married to him. He was scared, and he said that his wife was not being prudent to take him to the hospital where her lover worked and consult the doctor who was in fact her lover to take care of him. Brother

Bill said that he was not aware of the love affair his wife was having with the doctor. Today, he believes that God, by his grace, revealed his wife's secret love affair to him. He was amazed.

I believe Brother Bill's story because I had a similar experience in a relationship. For example, when I was engaged to a man I trusted, but he was not faithful to some extent. The Lord by His grace revealed to me about his love affair with one of my friends. When I confronted him, he denied it first; but later, he admitted that it was true. What caught my attention was the way we recognized God's mercy for us. As we were not living in the same country, my then fiancé, was surprised and he accepted that the Lord revealed his secret love affair. I am thankful to the Lord because He sees everything that I could not see. God's omniscient nature means, He knows and sees everything: "Nothing in all creation is hidden from God's sights" [Hebrews 4:12].

The interesting thing in all these stories is that there is room for compassion and forgiveness. As the people involved knew the Lord, there was room for humility, compassion, repentance, and forgiveness and to glorify the Lord.

Although cases of faithfulness and infidelity in relationships can be complicated, they are matters of the hearts and only God knows people's hearts. Only God sees peoples' thoughts. When God shows you something, don't doubt Him, trust Him because God does not lie. In most cases, when God reveals something regarding a relationship, you can be sure that something is not right and that it needs to be repaired. I remember when a friend was excited to get married after having failed in other relationships and had been divorced more than once, he was very happy about his third marriage, and sharing his joy with friends and relatives. Then, one day, I saw something strange, that I believe the Lord pointed out to me to share with him. This was regarding his new relationship. I approached him and we discussed. During our conversations, I remember, seeing my friend, admiring the love of God for him and he stated: "God must be talking to you, there are things, I have not shared with my fiancée. I need to share these things with her before I take her to the alter"" She needs to know about my past, I need to tell her this. My friend was thankful that the LORD knows him and He was taking care of him. Whatever message he needed to share with his fiancée before she said "I do" ONLY God knows because God knows and sees the thoughts in our hearts.

In another scenario, I had just started a romantic relationship, a heart captivating, smiles, jokes, and kindness, sort of things, a woman wishes to find in a loving man. As I started praying to the Lord about the relationship, a few days later, the Lord revealed that the man was in another relationship. I could not believe it. But since I truly believe that the Lord knows everything, sees everything and speaks in miraculous ways, I decided to remain quiet and observe. Sure enough, it became clear that my friend was in a romantic relationship, and it did not seem to bother him to start another romantic relationship.

This may not be a problem to some people who see things differently concerning friendship, love, and betrayal. To people who believe in honesty, truth, ant trust as characteristics among the criteria for friendship and a serious relationship, this is a problem because seeking to engage in more than one romantic relationship at the same time can lead to lies, dishonesty, and even murders, and horrible tragedies to some extent. When one engages in multiple romantic relationships, there can often be lies and confusion. Sooner or later the truth will come into the light. God's commands us to love and to forgive. We must do unto others as we wish to be done to us, this is the Lord's teaching. In Scriptures, there is a story of a man who gave his wife to a king because of fear. He lied to the king by saying that his wife was his sister, but God revealed to the king that he was taking someone else's wife. The king woke up with great fear. He confronted the man and he returned his wife to him:

> But God came to Abimelek in a dream one night and said to him, "You are as good as dead because of the woman you have taken; she is a married woman" [Genesis 20:3].

The man who lied to the King was Abraham. He gave his wife Sarah to King Abimelek. This story is found in Scriptures, in the Book of Genesis, chapter 3 from verse 1 to 17. As we read the story, one may say that Abraham did not lie because he was related to his wife Sarah. I took this story as an example to emphasize the fact that God is omniscient, He is all knowing and He sees everything.

I believe that God knows everything and He sees everything. The Lord Jesus told the woman at the well that the man he was living with was not her husband. The Lord knew about this because He is God, Our Creator.

These stories are told for God's glory. By His grace, He helps us to love and to forgive others.

God sees everything and He knows everything.

Speaking from experience, I can recall, a very painful, and sad tragedy that occurred to my family when my elder brother André Tshibamba Mundeke Chico was kidnapped and was brutally murdered in the middle of the night in Kinshasa in the Democratic Republic of the Congo, in Africa where we lived. My beloved brother André went out with his friends one evening. He was in a bar and people saw him being threatened with a knife in the bar; he never came back home alive. My beloved brother, poor André was kidnapped, in the middle of the night, he was beaten to death before he was shot several times, and his body was thrown in the street and left to die. The murderers staged the scene to make us believe that my beloved brother André was hit by a car. They wanted us to believe that he was in a car accident while he was brutally murdered with several bullets on his body. My beloved brother André was brutally murdered and some people knew about the murder plot. They even saw him being threatened with a knife in a bar as I already mentioned, but no one told my family and I about the reason my beloved brother André was threatened and shown a knife in the bar, nor about the murder plot. This is a painful and a tragic event that I don't want to think about or to recall, but I am recalling it here to glorify God for His amazing grace and for His Omniscient nature.

While my family members and my relatives were trying to figure out what happened to my beloved brother André, as we were panicking, crying, and trying to avenge the situation by taking matters into our own hands; God, by His amazing grace and mercy reached out to us and revealed that my beloved brother André was not murdered by his friends. God, by His amazing grace revealed to us that my beloved brother André was murdered by people he did not know, not by his friends. The Lord also provided a clear description of the murder scene, explaining how the murderers were dressed. Who could know that my beloved brother André was murdered by the people he did not know, but God Himself who created my beloved brother André and WHO knew him! God, by His amazing love gave us this message. About three or two days after the tragedy, the Lord exposed the murder plot.

After my family received this powerful revelation, a hidden secret regarding my brother's murder, my family decided that the case against my brother's murder be dismissed and that his friends be released from jail. They were arrested when we heard about the tragedy. Some people knew about the plot to murder my beloved brother André, but they did not want to tell us. But God Who knows and Who sees everything, showed His amazing grace to us and He gave us the grace to surrender all to HIM. The message was clear, my beloved brother André was murdered by people he did not know, not his friends. The information about the way the murderers were dressed was also something that only the Lord could know because He was there and He saw everything. Two or three years later, as we were still grieving for the loss of our dear and beloved brother André, the Lord Jesus Christ manifested His grace and mercy for my family. As one of my siblings listened to a chilling story of the murder of my beloved brother André, an handsome young man who was kidnapped in the middle of the night, was beaten up to death and shot several time by soldiers. The Lord sees everything and He confirms what He reveals.

By God's grace, we surrendered all to Him and we relied on Him. The tragedy hit home. We left Zaire, the Democratic Republic of the Congo, with the exception of my siblings who were married. It did not take long, God showed us His mercy and compassion as people who knew or heard something about our tragedy started talking; and those who were involved in the murder plot to murder my beloved brother André started fighting among themselves and some died in car accidents. I tell these stories to give God glory and to testify to His Omniscience and Omnipresence nature and to testify that the Lord God is our Lord and Savior Jesus Christ.

These stories I have just related are painful and disturbing, Only by God's grace am I able to recall them and to write about them for God's glory. God's love and mercy help us to love and to forgive; to love those who have wronged us. My prayers and wishes for those who hurt my family is that they know the Lord Jesus Christ and accept Him as their Savior. Scriptures instruct us that God loves us and He wants the world to be saved:

> For God so loved the world that he gave his one and only Son, that whoever believes in him shall not perish but have eternal life. [17] For God did not send his Son into the world to condemn the world, but to save the world through him. [18] Whoever believes in him is not condemned, but whoever does not believe stands condemned already because they have not believed in the name of God's one and only Son. [19] This is the verdict: Light has come into the world, but people loved darkness instead of light because their deeds were evil. [20] Everyone who does evil hates the light, and will not come into the light for fear that their deeds will be exposed. [21] But whoever lives by the truth comes into the light, so that it may be seen plainly that what they have done has been done in the sight of God [John 3:16-21].

When people know the Lord, they will fear God. My advice to anyone who has experienced the unthinkable tragic event is to surrender it all to God and to pray to God for grace, mercy, peace, a forgiving heart and healing. Nothing is hidden from God's sights. He knows everything and He sees everything.

Regarding love affairs, confrontations, and discussions, it is important to indicate that when the Lord revealed a hidden secret to a partner, there is a blessing for all those involved. I believe that the Lord gives a chance to each person to clean up his or her acts; because the one who is confronted becomes aware that God sees everything he or she does, and the one who confronts is convinced that God sees everything and if he or she does something wrong, the Lord can expose it as well. There are lessons to be learned for all the people involved. Honesty and truth are characteristics for a healthy relationship. Do unto other what you wish to be done to you. This is a well-known lesson in the teachings of Our Lord and Savior Jesus Christ: Do to others as you would have them do to you" [Luk2 6:31].

The Omniscient God WHO knows and sees everything can expose the hidden secrets. God is everywhere and He sees everything. Nothing in all creation is hidden from God's sight.

Scriptures teach us that, God is omniscient. He knows and He sees everything. Scriptures also teach us that the Lord Jesus Christ is Omniscient, He knows and He sees everything. He knew peoples' thoughts as we read in Scriptures:

> Now while he was in Jerusalem at the Passover Festival, many people saw the signs he was performing and believed in his name. [d] 24 But Jesus would not entrust himself to them, for he knew all people. 25 He did not need any testimony about mankind, for he knew what was in each person [John 2:23-25].

This passage shows that the Lord Jesus Christ is God, He is Omniscient. He knows our thoughts and He sees them. As a matter of fact, the Lord perceives our thoughts from the distance as we read in the Book of Psalms [139:2].

Conclusion

To conclude, it is important to recall that the Lord Jesus Christ's attributes are the same attributes for God. For examples, the Lord Jesus Christ is omniscient because He knows people's thoughts and can tell the secrets of our hearts. God knows and sees everything. He knows the thoughts in our hearts. The Lord Jesus Christ is omnipresent, He is everywhere, He sees everything, and He knows everything. After His resurrection, the Lord was everywhere. He appeared in different places. To God be the glory. The Lord promised that He would be with us always till the end of the time [Matthew 28]. Finally, Scriptures provide us with powerful information about the attributes of God, our Creator, and they assert to us that there is Only ONE GOD and that He is Our Lord and Savior Jesus Christ. This message is very simple and clear, but at the same time, it is hidden because Only the Holy Spirit can open one's mind to understand it and to grasp the meaning. We know that Only the Holy Spirit can help us to understand spiritual things because in many circumstances, Scriptures instruct us that only God can help us to understand spiritual things. For examples, when Peter told the Lord Jesus Christ that He Is the Anointed one, the Messiah, the Lord said that His Father had revealed this to Peter. The Father is the Holy Spirit, the Holy Spirit is the Lord Jesus Christ, God, Our Creator. Scriptures instruct us that there is Only One God.

When you read about the Holy Spirit in such passages as Luke 1-34-38, when the angel announced the Birth of Our Lord and Savior Jesus Christ to Mary, and you compare to the passages of John 14: 15-21, when the Lord Jesus promises the Holy Spirit, you will notice that the Father, the Holy Spirit and the Lord Jesus Chris are ONE. The Lord said, "The *Father and I are One*" [John 10:30].

The apostle Paul instructs us that only spiritual people understand spiritual things. Therefore, we need the Holy Spirit to understand spiritually things, to understand the Lord's nature, and His attributes as they reveal that there is Only One God, He is Our Lord and Savior Jesus Christ.

Activities for this chapter

1. Recall verses that teach about God's omniscience.

   ____
   ____
   ____
   ____

2. Do you believe that God knows and sees everything?

   ____
   ____
   ____
   ____

3. If you do not believe that God knows and sees everything, provide your reasons.

   ____
   ____
   ____
   ____

4. Why do you believe so? Before you write down your reasons, please consider reading a few passages from the Scriptures, the inspired Word. As a suggestion, you may read the passages below:

    a. Hebrews 4:12
    b. Psalm 139.

    ____
    ____
    ____
    ____

CHAPTER 17

The Power and Authority of the Scriptures

> Then Jesus came to them and said, "All authority in heaven and on earth has been given to me. [19] Therefore go and make disciples of all nations, baptizing them in the name of the Father and of the Son and of the Holy Spirit, [20] and teaching them to obey everything I have commanded you. And surely I am with you always, to the very end of the age" [Matthew 28:18].

Why It is Important to Use Scriptures in the Discussions about Christ's Deity

Scriptures are the breathed Word of God [2 Timothy: 3:16]. They instruct us about God. Moreover, Scriptures have absolute authority, therefore it makes sense to use more passages from the Scriptures in the Holy Bible to discuss such complex topics as the Deity of the Lord Jesus Christ, His Incarnation when he comes to earth for His Second coming to take us with him as He went to earth to prepare a place for us [John 14:1]. As we can remember, the Lord Jesus Christ came to earth for the first time through the Virgin birth [Matthew 1-1]. He came to redeem us from the curse that was caused by the Fall of Man as we read in the Book of Genesis, chapter 3. Now, to discuss Christ's Deity, His ministry, His crucifixion, and His resurrection from the dead, we need to refer to Scriptures. All these remarkable events are well addressed and explained in the Scriptures. Therefore, if one wishes to learn about God's existence, His nature, His creation, and His commands, one needs to consider the Scriptures in the Holy Bible.

The passages in the Scriptures are clear and they have authority because Scriptures are the inspired Word of God [2 Timothy 3:16]. We are told that God is the Word: "In the beginning was the Word, and the Word was with God, and the Word was God." [John 1:1]. Now, if you don't use Scriptures to address facts and to discuss spiritual events, how would you possibly support your statements? If you wish to learn about the Creator, His attributes and His nature, you must consider Scriptures to read them, and cite them without human interpretation. In addition to learning about creation, to discuss creation and the origin of life from spiritual perspectives, one needs to examine the Scriptures because it is in the Scriptures that we find more information about the Creator and His creation:

> In the beginning was the Word, and the Word was with God, and the Word was God. [2] He was with God in the beginning. [3] Through him all things were made; without him nothing was made that has been made. [4] In him was life, and that life was the light of all mankind. [5] The light shines in the darkness, and the darkness has not overcome[a] it [John1:1-5].

As you can notice, the passage above teaches us more about God, Our Creator, His existence, His nature, and His Creation. Similarly, the passage teaches us about how the Lord created the world and about His coming to earth when He took on Flesh. How could you possibly tell people that God took on Flesh to become Man, came to earth and lived among people without supporting these statements by using powerful verses from the Word of God?

Nobody knows more about God than God Himself, and God speaks to us through His Word. It is true that God can speak to us in many ways including through His Son, His Voice, and through the prophets, through dreams and visions and Through His Son [Hebrew 1:2]

Today, most people would agree that the most common way that God uses to speak to many people is through His Word in in the Holy Bible. A glance at history and social life reveals that the Holy Bible is the most translated and the most read Book in the world.

When I first heard that the Bible is the most translated and the most read Book in the world, it did not say much to me at that moment. Even when I heard this for the second time, and even the third time, it did not say much to me, and I was not surprised neither. However, as time passed and as I started writing this book, *My Lord and My God,* I realized the magnitude of the subject I am writing about and the importance of the Scriptures. I realized that I could not support my statement that the Lord Jesus Christ is God, Our Creator, our Lord, our Savior, our Redeemer, and our King without citing the Scriptures. In other words, to discuss God's existence and His attributes, one needs to draw from Scriptures. One needs God's guidance.

Have you ever wondered why the Bible is the most translated and the most read Book in the world? The answer is that Scriptures in the Holy Bible are the Word of God. Among many other reasons one can present, the clear and simple answer is that Scriptures are the Word of God. The Word of God does not change because God does not change, as it is written, "Jesus Christ is the same yesterday, today and forever "[Hebrew 13:8]. People can interpret Scriptures in the Holy Bible as they wish, but the Word of God remains unchanged, permanent, irreversible, undeniable, indisputable, immutable, final, and absolute. In other word, the Word of God cannot be changed. All the adjectives that describe absolute truth and unchanged are applied to the Word of God. For this reason, there is a need for one to cite the Word of God when one writes about God's truth. The Truth is that God exists and there is Only One God, Our Lord and Savior Jesus Christ who is immutable, He does not change because He is God.

God speaks truth to us through His Word, and He guides us through His Word. Consider, the truth of God concerning murder and adultery, for example, God has provided us with His commands. The Word of God teaches us that God commands us not to Kill. "Thou Shall Not Kill," No matter how people have tried to interpret what is murder, what is not murder, and why one should do this and that, the Word of God remains clear about murder: "Thou Shall Not Kill." Another example of God's commands is about adultery. The Word of God condemns adultery, Regardless of man's interpretation about adultery, as some seek to explain when and why a man can take someone else's spouse, the Word of God remains clear; God hates adultery and God hates divorce.

God Is Love [1 John 4:8]. Regardless of what men think or do, God Is love. He will not change. Love Is God's nature and He will not change His character despite men's disobedience and sinful nature. You know what I am talking about because we are all sinners saved by grace.

Scriptures teach that if someone says that they don't sin, they are liar: "*If we claim to be without sin, we deceive ourselves and the truth is not in us* "[I John 1:8].

How many times have we sinned throughout the day, and yet, the Lord God still loves us and Is patient with us, and He still reaches out to us?

I remember when the unthinkable tragedy hit my family On July 8, 1982 when my dear beloved brother, André Tshibamba Mundeke Chico was murdered in the middle of the night out of jealousy by people he did not know in the Democratic Republic of Congo, the former Zaire. I have recorded this tragic incident in my precious writings when discussing the feelings of sadness and vengeance. Because of the evil nature of the tragedy, I often recall this tragic incident with pain and sadness. The sadness, the pain and the psychological trauma the tragedy has caused me are indescribable only by God's grace I am able to write about this. What I mean here is that it was very difficult for me to think about forgiveness for the people who murdered my brother for many years. I believed in vengeance by the Lord, but I could not think about forgiveness for many years. I suffered anger, sadness, and unforgiving heart until the Lord by His mercy assisted me and little by little I started thinking that if the people who murdered my brother accepted the Lord Jesus Christ as their personal Savior, maybe this could help me to start thinking about forgiving them. This was the beginning, I surrendered all to the Lord.

It was a nightmare, because even in my dreams, I would see people telling me, "we are the ones who murdered your brother. What are you going to do to us?" At that point, I made up my mind to forgive the people who murdered my beloved brother André, and I surrender all to the Lord, because the lack of forgiveness can be a sin; I am glad the Lord took the heavy Lord away. This does not mean that I have forgotten the tragic event that his my family. I think about my brother André constantly, but I turn to the Lord for peace.

The Name of Immanuel Means God with us

Take for example, the name of the Lord Jesus Christ, "Immanuel." The name Immanuel means God with us as Scriptures instruct us: *"The virgin will conceive and give birth to a son, and they will call him Immanuel" (which means "God with us*") [Matthew 1:23]. Frankly, with such clear instructions and explanations, there is no need to question Christ's Deity or to doubt that the Lord Jesus Christ is God, our Creator because when we believe in Scriptures, we have to believe the teaching we receive from the Lord. It is surprising to notice that some people question Christ's Deity even after they have read the passages that explain the Lord's name, Immanuel. A closer examination of the Scriptures reveals that there is ONLY ONE God, He hates idolatry and He does not give His glory to another, as we read in such passages as Isaiah 48:2: "*I am the LORD; that is my name! I will not yield my glory to another or my praise to idols.*" Now, as the name Immanuel means God is with us, and as God does not give His glory to another, it is logical to conclude that the Lord God, Our Creator took on Flesh and came to earth to save us.

In addition, to the example of the name Immanuel that testifies to Christ's, we can also consider the work that the Lord Jesus accomplished; these numerous miracles that Only God could do. Among these miracles were the healing the sick, the forgiveness of sins, raising the dead, and raising Himself from death.

First, Scriptures instruct us that the Lord was worshiped. For examples, the Magi came to worship the Baby Jesus, Immanuel. This is remarkable and amazing because if the Lord Jesus Christ was not God, the Magi would not worship Him. If they did not recognize His power and authority, they would not have worshipped Him. Moreover, if the Baby Immanuel was not God in the flesh, then God would not have allowed the magi to worship Him because God does not share His glory with another. If God allowed the magi to worship the Baby Jesus, Immanuel, this means that the Baby Jesus, Immanuel was God Himself in the Flesh as His name explains "Immanuel, God with us." [Matthew 1:21-23].

Secondly, because God hates idolatry, He could not allow the Magi to worship the Baby Jesus, Immanuel when He was born and even when He grew up, doing ministry on earth.

Most Christians know that only God can be worshipped and that during His earthly ministry, the Lord Jesus Christ accepted to be worshipped. The fact that people worshipped the Lord Jesus Christ, and the Lord accepted worship from angels and from people is very critical in the discussions about Christ's Deity because Only God, our Creator Is to be worshipped. As the Lord Jesus Christ accepts worship, the Lord Jesus- Christ is God, Our Creator.

Furthermore, when we consider that the Lord's name Immanuel means God with us, it makes perfect sense because Scriptures instruct us that, in Christ dwelt the fullness of the Deity as we read: "*For in Christ all the fullness of the Deity lives in bodily form,*" [Colossians 2:9]. It can be difficult to imagine that the fullness of the Deity lived in Christ because our human capacity cannot comprehend all spiritual mysteries. We are limited in our ability, we need to have faith in God and to believe in Him. Faith is a gift from God, and without faith it is impossible to please God" *For it is by grace you have been saved, through faith--and this is not from yourselves, it is the gift of God* "[Ephesians 2:8]. There is a need to have faith in God in order to understand spiritual things. A spiritual man understands spiritual things while a carnal man cannot understand spiritual things as discussed in the Book of Romans: *"The person without the Spirit does not accept the things that come from the Spirit of God but considers them foolishness, and cannot understand them because they are discerned only through the Spirit"* [1 Corinthians 2:14].

When one reads that the Lord Jesus Christ is Immanuel, God with us, one needs the Spirit of God in order to understand this amazing truth and powerful mystery. Without the Spirit of God, one cannot understand God's truth and spiritual mysteries. Similarly, one cannot worship God in truth unless that person has the Spirit of God. It is written: "God Is Spirit, and his worshipers must worship in the Spirit and in truth" [John 4:24]. When someone finds it hard to believe that there is Only One God and that He Is the Lord Jesus Christ, maybe the best place to start is to pray to God for assistance and to ask Him for faith in Him because when one believes in God, and is willing to love God and to obey His commandments, the Spirit of God will guide him or her in truth because God is Truth.

Scriptures teach us that God is Truth: "*Sanctify them by the truth; your word is truth*" [John17:17]. Scriptures also teach us that the Lord Jesus Christ is Truth: "*Jesus answered, "I am the way and the truth and the life. No one comes to the Father except through me* [John 14:6]. The message is clear, God is Truth and the Lord Jesus Christ is Truth. This should not cause a problem because there is Only One God" "Hear, O Israel: The LORD our God, the LORD is one" [Deuteronomy 6:4]. Scriptures also teach us that God is the Word and the Word became Flesh and dwelt among men: "*In the beginning was the Word, and the Word was with God, and the Word was God. [2] He was with God in the beginning. [3] Through him all things were made; without him nothing was made that has been made. [4] In him was life, and that life was the light of all mankind. [5] The light shines in the darkness, and the darkness has not overcome[a] it*: [John 1:2], Now, when one refuses to accept the fundamental truth that there is Only One God, Our Creator, as Scriptures instruct us, one will not understand that the Lord Jesus Christ is God, Our Creator as it is written that God is the Word and God took on Flesh and became Man and lived among us [1:1-14].. Believing in God and obeying His Word is a matter of faith and trust for it is by faith in God that we believe that the universe was formed by God at His Command: "*By faith we understand that the universe was formed at God's command, so that what is seen was not made out of what was visible*" [Hebrews 11:6].

Believing in God alone is not sufficient. One needs to believe in God and be willing to obey His commands as Scriptures teach us that the demons also believe in God and tremble:" You believe that there is one God. Good! Even the demons believe that--and shudder" [James: 9]. Based on this discussion, one can see the importance of faith in God and obedience to God's commands. When one believes in God and does not trust God or obey HIM, one will not be in harmony with the Lord. In other words, when one says that he or she believes in God the Father, but does not believe that God the Father and the Lord Jesus Christ are ONE as the Lord Jesus Christ stated, one makes a serious error. The Lord stated that He and the Father are ONE: "I and the Father are one" [John 10:30]. The Lord also stated that He who sees Him has seen the Father: Philip said, "Lord, show us the Father and that will be enough for us." [9] Jesus answered: "Don't you know me, Philip, even after I have been among you such a long time? Anyone who has seen me has seen the Father. How can you say, 'Show us the Father'? [John 14:8-9]. Moreover, the Lord also stated that before Abraham was, He IS. He also stated: [24] I told you that you would die in your sins; if you do not believe that I am he, you will indeed die in your sins"[John 8:24]. These are the significant facts to consider in the discussions about the Deity of the Lord Jesus Christ.

Now, if one does not believe in what the Lord Jesus Christ Himself states, it will be difficult for one to understand Christ's Deity because to understand Christ's Deity is a matter of faith in Christ. You need to believe in Him.

Another passage in the Bible worth mentioning in the discussions about Christ's Deity to recall is the passage that recalls the Lord Jesus Christ's responses to the Devil when the later tried to tempt Him by leading Him into the wilderness as there was an exchange of words between the Lord Jesus Christ and the Devil during this critical time. Scriptures inform us that the Lord Jesus told Satan that He created him:

> [6] *"If you are the Son of God," he said, "throw yourself down. For it is written:*
>
> *"'He will command his angels concerning you,*
> *and they will lift you up in their hands,*
> *so that you will not strike your foot against a stone.[c]'"*
>
> [7] *Jesus answered him, "It is also written: 'Do not put the Lord your God to the test"[Matthew 4:6:7].*

Now, as the Lord Jesus Christ Himself tells Satan that He is God who created Him, this should settle the matter about Christ's Deity.

Finally, when the Lord said that He is the Son of Man, they wanted to kill Him because the Son of God IS God Himself. This discussion should instruct us that the Lord Jesus Christ is God because there is Only One God. If the Lord Jesus Christ was not God, our Creator, He would not have accepted to go to the cross to be crucified to pay the price for our sins, to experience death to save us and to raise Himself from the dead so that we can have eternal life. Let us remember that the Lord said that because He lives, we will also live [Matthew 14:19]. How can the Lord give us life if He is not God, our Creator, the Author of life? The Lord teaches us that He came so that we can have life in abundance [John 10:10]. The Lord came to give us life. He bought our salvation with His Precious Blood, the Blood of God [Acts 20:28].

Scriptures teach us that the Lord Jesus Christ is the Author of life: "You killed the author of life, but God raised him from the dead. We are witnesses of this" [Acts 3:15]. This is an important indication that the Lord is God, Our Creator.

Scriptures clearly teach us that in the Beginning was the Word and the Word was with God and the Word was God as we read in the Book of John 1:2: In the beginning was the Word, and the Word was with God, *and the Word was God.* [2] He was with God in the beginning." This powerful verse does not need an interpretation.

Also, we read that everything was made through and that nothing was made that has been made, it is clear that the Lord Jesus Christ is God, our Creator, who created you and me because nothing was made without Him. All was made through Him:

> [3] Through him all things were made; without him nothing was made that has been made. [4] In him was life, and that life was the light of all mankind. [5] The light shines in the darkness, and the darkness has not overcome[a] it [John 1:3].

The passages above clearly informs us that the Lord Jesus Christ Is God, Our Creator.

All these passages from the Scriptures do not need interpretations. When men start interpreting the Scriptures, there is room for errors and mistakes. Most passages in the Scriptures that teach us about the Lord Jesus Christ's Deity are not too complicated, as we read in the passages above. "The Word was with God and the Word was God." What is it here to interpret? Clearly, nothing! Furthermore, we read that "through Him all things were made, and that without him nothing was made that has been made." What is needs to be interpreted? Which words or sentences need to be analyzed? Clearly none.

After reading the passages above about Our Lord's Deity, one can rightly state that Scriptures clearly instruct us that the Lord Jesus Christ Is God, Our Creator. After considering few passages about the Lord's Deity as God, Our Creator, one can state that the Word of God is clear about Christ's Deity because there is Only One God who is the Savior and the Almighty, Lord Jesus Christ. All these titles and attributes are His.

The Lord has all authority, in heaven and on earth because all things were created by Him and for Him as we read in Scriptures:

> **The Supremacy of the Son of God**
>
> The Son is the image of the invisible God, the firstborn over all creation. [16] For in him all things were created: things in heaven and on earth, visible and invisible, whether thrones or powers or rulers or authorities; all things have been created through him and for him. [17] He is before all things, and in him all things hold together. [18] And he is the head of the body, the church; he is the beginning and the firstborn from among the dead, so that in everything he might have the supremacy. [19] For God was pleased to have all his fullness dwell in him, [20] and through him to reconcile to himself all things, whether things on earth or things in heaven, by making peace through his blood, shed on the cross [Colossians 1:15].

Let us also remember that prior to ascending to heaven, the Lord Jesus Christ commanded us to make all people His disciples and He stated that all authority on earth and in heaven has been given to Him: "All authority in heaven and on earth had been given to me. [19] Therefore go and make disciples of all nations, baptizing them in the name of the Father and of the Son and of the Holy Spirit, [20] and teaching them to obey everything I have commanded you. And surely I am with you always, to the very end of the age" [Matthew 28:18-20].

Activities for this Chapter

1. Write down two passages that teach you about the truth of the Word of God.

    ____
    ____
    ____
    ____

2. Which names of the Lord Jesus Christ teach you the most about His attributes as the Creator of the universe?

    ____
    ____
    ____
    ____

3. Make a list of the names of the Lord Jesus Christ and His attributes and underline the attributes of the Lord that you think minister to you the most about His Deity as God, our Creator, your creator and my creator.

    ____
    ____
    ____
    ____

CONCLUSION

> I said therefore to you, that you shall die in your sins; for unless you believe that I am He, you shall die in your sins" [John 8:24].

In conclusion, there is a need to refer to Scriptures in the Holy Bible in order to discuss the Deity of Our Lord and Savior Jesus Christ. As Scriptures teach us that there is Only One God as we read many verses in the Old Testament and many verses in the New Testament, it is important to examine them as they show that the Lord Jesus Christ is God, our Creator. For this reason, certain passages such as the ones in Deuteronomy (6:4); and the ones in Isaiah [9:6] are very important to consider. In addition, the passages of John 1-1-5; and Colossians 1:1-15 are very important.

My Lord and My God has considered several passages from the Scriptures to address Christ's Deity and to show that the Lord Jesus Christ Is God, Our Creator. He took on flesh and He came to earth to save us. Christ's Deity is clearly explained in Scriptures. The Lord Jesus Christ is God, our Creator and Scriptures clearly teach us about this powerful truth. The Lord Jesus Christ Himself teaches us that there is Only One God and He is God our Creator. How can one possibly fail to grasp this powerful message in the powerful passages of the Scriptures including Deuteronomy 6:4: "Hear, O Israel: The LORD our God, the LORD is one"; and the passage in John 10:30: "I and the Father are ONE?" Also, the passage of [John 8:24]: "I told you that you would die in your sins; if you do not believe that I am he, you will indeed die in your sins." is worthy considering in the discussions about Christ's Deity.

Anyone who believes in the Scriptures, will agree that they are the inspired Word of God: All Scripture is God-breathed and is useful for teaching, rebuking, correcting and training in righteousness, [2 Timothy 3:16]; they instruct us about God, and they are the truth as our Lord stated:

"Sanctify them by the truth; your word is truth" [John17:17]. The evidence to God's existence, His power and His oneness is clearly declared in the Scriptures. *My Lord and My God* has presented many passages that teach about Christ's Deity to confirm that there is Only One God and that He is Our Lord and Savior Jesus Christ. Some passages have been presented separately and others have been presented in bulk or in groups as they have been compiled by other scholars.

Scriptures speak about the Lord Jesus Christ as Our Creator and Our Savior. The entire Bible speaks about the LORD Jesus Christ. Due to publications rules that have imposed a reduction of Biblical citations, *this book has used most popular passages that speak about the Lord Jesus Christ.*

Although My Lord and My God has presented a great amount of Biblical passages that instruct us about Christ Deity, there are many passages from the Scriptures that have been left out due to publications rules that have imposed a reduction of Biblical citations. I urge the audience to search the Scriptures and to read more passages about Christ's Deity. An examination of more passages from the Scriptures helps to remove doubt about Christ's Deity because there is Only One God; He is Our Creator, He loves us and He came to earth to save us. He is the Lord Jesus Christ, He is the Way, the Truth and the Life, No One goes to the Father except through HIM, as He said [John 14:6].

Moreover, in Scriptures, we also read that Salvation is Only in Christ:

> Salvation is found in no one else, for there is no other name under heaven given to mankind by which we must be saved" [Acts 4:12].

In conclusion, let us take a glance at the Lord's words of grace compassion as He invites us to HIM:

> Here I am! I stand at the door and knock. If anyone hears my voice and opens the door, I will come in and eat with that person, and they with me [Revelation 3:20].

God exists, He is our Creator. God created us in His image. God spoke the world into to existence. God became Man to save us after the fall of man as we read in the Book of Genesis [Genesis 3]. After the Fall of Man, God decided to save the world, He took on Flesh and He came to earth. When God came to earth, He was called Immanuel, God with us. He also took the name of Jesus, He lived among men and He preached the good news. He then went to the cross to pay the price to redeem us and to cleanse us with His Precious Blood. The Precious Blood of Jesus washes away our sins.

The Precious Blood of Our Lord Jesus Christ removed the Original Sin from our records. The Precious Blood of our Lord Jesus Christ removed the curse on the world. The Precious Blood of Our Lord Jesus Christ brought reconciliation between men and God.

The Lord Jesus Christ is God, our Creator.

The Lord Jesus Christ is God, Our Creator. There is salvation in No other name.

> Salvation is found in no one else, for there is no other name under heaven given to mankind by which we must be saved" [Acts 4:12].

Also, we read in John 1:16-17: [16] Simon Peter answered, "You are the Messiah, the Son of the living God."

> Jesus replied, "Blessed are you, Simon son of Jonah, for this was not revealed to you by flesh and blood, but by my Father in heaven [John17:17.

Please refer to the Scriptures and read more about Christ's Deity. Although My Lord and My God has presented a good number of passages about Christ's Deity, there are many other powerful passages in the Scriptures. As I mentioned before, due to the publication restrictions, *My Lord and My God* has left out many passages about Christ's Deity. The Lord Jesus Christ is described as King of kings and Lord of lords. He is also described as Eternal God and all-knowing. A study of the Lord's title as Eternal God is worth considering.

Also, the Lord has many titles and names, examining the Lord's names and titles helps us to see that the Lord Jesus Christ is God. Our Creator.

The Holy Bible contains 66 books. In each Book of the Bible there is mention of God because Scriptures instruct us about God touching on a variety of subjects including, God's nature, God's attributes, God's deeds God's names, God's commands, and God's will for us. When you think about God's magnificence and the numerous subjects regarding His Holy Name, you will soon realize that this book, *My Lord and God* has recalled only a few passages from the Bible that speak about Christ's Deity because the Lord Jesus Christ is God our Creator. He came down to save us, to forgive our Original Sin and to give us life. There is Only One God, as we read:

> I am the LORD, and there is no other; apart from me there is no God. I will strengthen you, though you have not acknowledged me [Isaiah 45:5].
>
> I, even I, am the LORD, and apart from me there is no savior [Isaiah 43:11].

In conclusion, please refer to the Scriptures as they present numerous passages that instruct us that there is Only One God and that He is the Lord Jesus Christ.

The Lord Himself says that there is no other God, but Him, as He instructs us:

> I am the LORD, and there is no other; apart from me there is no God. I will strengthen you, though you have not acknowledged me [Isaiah 45:5]
>
> I told you that you would die in your sins; if you do not believe that I am he, you will indeed die in your sins" [John 8:24].
>
> Hear, O Israel: The LORD our God, the LORD is one [Deuteronomy 6:4].

REFERENCES

Annie Ngana- Mundeke, Christ's Deity. Iuniverse. Bloomington, Indiana, the United States. 2010

Annie .Ngana-Mundeke. Creation: And God Said, "Let There Be Light." Iuniverse, New York, Bloomington, the United States. 2011

John Morris: Noah's Ark and the Ararat Adventure. Master Books. USA. 1994

Tim Keller: The Reason for God: Belief in an Age of Skepticism. Dulton. The United States 2008

Matt Slick: Jesus is God. CARM. The United States. 2009

A.R Torrey: New Topical Textbook. The United States. 1897

The King James Bible. Great Britain. Europe. 1611

The Holy Bible, New International Version. Grand Rapids: Zondervan House, 1984

The New American Standard Bible (NASB). The Lockman Foundation. USA. 1971

ABOUT THE AUTHOR

Dr. Annie Ngana-Mundeke is a writer who has written books about religious subjects including: *Creation: The Power of the Word of God and Evidence to Creation; Christ's Deity; The Gifts Everyone Needs, the Gift Everyone will use; Free Healing From God: Do You Believe; Creation and God Said: Let There Be Light; Jesus Love Children Vol.1; Jesus Loves Children Vol. 2 and the Big Nails.*

Annie is an educator. She has authored and edited books that address various social issues such as *The Monstrous Tragedy of September 11 and Healing Process.*

Printed in the United States
By Bookmasters